Let us therefore come boldly unto
the throne of grace, that we may obtain mercy,
and find grace to help in time of need.

HEBREWS 4:16 KJV

The main lesson about prayer is just this:
Do it! Do it! Do it!

JOHN LAIDLAW

The Pocket Guide for Parents: Praying with & for Your Kids

Copyright © 2006 by Bordon Books

Product developed by Bordon Books, Tulsa, Oklahoma.
Writing and compilation by Deborah Webb, Betsy Williams, and Rebecca Currington in association with SnapdragonGroup℠ Editorial Services.
Cover design by Thinkpen Designs.

Published by Bethany House Publishers
11400 Hampshire Avenue South
Bloomington, Minnesota 55438

Bethany House Publishers is a division of
Baker Publishing Group, Grand Rapids, Michigan.

Printed in the United States of America
ISBN-13: 978-0-7642-0224-7
ISBN-10: 0-7642-0224-3

Also available from Bethany House Publishers
The Pocket Guide for Parents: Raising Godly Kids

Library of Congress Cataloging-in-Publication Data
The pocket guide for parents : praying with and for your kids.
    p. cm.
Summary: "This compact parenting book will help parents practice the discipline of prayer as they teach their children the power of prayer. Sample prayers for specific situations and ages of children will assist the parent to pray for—and with—their kids, from toddlers through teens"—Provided by publisher.
  ISBN-13: 978-0-7642-0224-7 (pbk.)
  ISBN-10: 0-7642-0224-3 (pbk.)
  1. Parents—Prayer-books and devotions—English. 2. Prayer—Christianity. I. Bethany House Publishers.

BV4845.P63 2007
249—dc22   2006027945

THE
P🏠CKET
GUIDE *for*
PARENTS

Praying with & for Your Kids

BETHANYHOUSE
MINNEAPOLIS, MINNESOTA

Introduction

Parenting is one of the toughest challenges we face here on earth. A human life, created in God's own image, is given to us to protect, nurture, and educate, all the while knowing that both failure and success will have eternal consequences. But God never meant for us to attempt it alone. He has provided us with second-by-second access to His throne room. His Word states that all we have to do is come and ask, and His vast resources will be made available to us. He truly is there for us, no matter how great or small our needs might be.

The Pocket Guide for Parents: Praying with & for Your Kids was created to assist you as you practice the power of prayer in your life and the lives of your children. Not only will it help you successfully navigate the tough times together, but it will also help your children develop the greatest life skill possible—a personal relationship with God through prayer. Important insights about the types of prayer and attitudes needed for effective prayer have been included, as well as specific need-based prayers to pray together. There are also Bible prayers that will teach you how to pray in certain accordance with God's Word.

Parenting is not for the faint of heart, but for the Christian parent, God provides all that is necessary to succeed.

The Soul of a Child

The soul of a child is the loveliest flower
That grows in the Garden of God;
Its climb is from weakness to knowledge and power,
To the sky from the clay and the sod.

To beauty and sweetness it grows under care,
Neglected, 'tis ragged and wild.
'Tis a plant that is tender but wondrously rare,
The sweet, wistful soul of a child.

Be tender, O gardener, and give it its share
Of moisture, of warmth, and of light,
And let it not lack for thy painstaking care
To protect it from frost and from blight.

A glad day will come when its bloom shall unfold,
It will seem that an angel has smiled,
Reflecting its beauty and sweetness untold,
In the sensitive heart of a child.

AUTHOR UNKNOWN

Contents

I. Strapping on the Wings of Prayer

II. Choosing a Holy Destination

III. Flying High Overhead

IV. Avoiding a Loss of Altitude

V. Prayers to Pray with Your Children

Prayers for the Heart of Your Toddler

Prayers for the Heart of Your Elementary-Aged Child

Prayers for the Heart of Your Teen

VI. Prayers for Your Child's Specific Needs

Prayers for the Needs of Your Toddler

Prayers for the Needs of Your Elementary-Aged Child

Prayers for the Needs of Your Teen

VII. Scripture Prayers

Our own personal experience
can never be taken as the norm for other people.
What matters is that our prayers should be living
and sincere. Each of us has his own temperament;
one is more intuitive, another more logical;
one is more intellectual, another more emotional.
The relationship of each with God will be marked
with the stamp of his own particular temperament.

PAUL TOURNIER

It is true friendship to teach one another to pray.
It is a believing [parent's] part to teach their
little children to pray. But the Holy Spirit's
love is greater than this. He not only puts
the words in our mouth, but He puts
the desire in our heart.

Robert Murray M'Cheyne

Strapping on the Wings of Prayer

All About Prayer

**Devote yourselves to prayer,
being watchful and thankful.**

COLOSSIANS 4:2

16

Be yourself. Be natural before God. Do not pretend to express emotions you do not feel. Tell Him whatever is on your heart and mind with whatever words are most natural to you. You do not have to speak to Him in "religious" language about "spiritual" matters only. Speak as naturally and as easily as you would to a friend, since God is just that.

John B. Coburn

A Place to Begin

**Let us then approach the throne of grace
with confidence, so that we may receive mercy
and find grace to help us in our time of need.**

HEBREWS 4:16

An elementary school-aged boy stood on the steps of the capitol building with his father, waiting. They were minutes away from a personal interview with the president of the United States. A local news reporter approached to tape a brief news clip just as the boy spotted a large Japanese beetle crawling along the pavement two stairs behind.

"Young man," the reporter began. "I hear you are about to meet the president."

"Yes sir," he said, nodding without looking up. He was obviously distracted with the bug.

"You *are* aware that he is the most powerful leader in the world, aren't you?"

"Sure," the boy said, seemingly unaffected.

"Are you excited?" the reporter pressed for a reaction.

The boy still didn't look up. "Sure, I guess."

"You'll get to shake his hand and speak to him, you know," the newsman continued.

"Yeah, I know."

"So, tell us something about what you're feeling. Are you nervous?"

The young boy finally glanced up from the ground. "Sir," he responded. "My father and I talked to God this morning. He created the whole *world*."

The privilege of prayer puts us in the presence of the most powerful *Being* in the world, in the galaxy, even in the realm of all eternity! What could any human being possibly have to say that He would be interested in hearing?

The eyes of the Lord are on the righteous and his ears are attentive to their prayer.

1 PETER 3:12

As staggering as it seems, the God of the universe is interested in knowing what is important to you—what occupies your heart. Prayer, you see, is the great privilege of speaking heart-to-heart with the Almighty. And likely, there will never be anything more pressing on your heart than your children.

Thankfully, because God is a Father, He can relate to your concerns for your children more than anyone. The reason He sent His own Son in the flesh was, in part, that He wanted to be able to empathize with you from your human frame of reference. Jesus' coming allowed Him to understand what it's like to be human, thus paving the way for you to speak to Him about anything and everything that confronts you from a human perspective.

The writer of the New Testament book of Hebrews put it this way:

We who have fled to him [Jesus] for refuge can take new courage, for we can hold on to his promise with confidence. This confidence is like a strong and trustworthy anchor for our souls. It leads us through the curtain of heaven into God's inner sanctuary. Jesus has already gone in there for us. . . . That is why we have a great High Priest who has gone to heaven, Jesus the Son of God (Hebrews 6:18–20; 4:14 NLT).

Jesus, as God in human flesh, became the Advocate and Intercessor on behalf of all people and has already entered the throne room on your behalf. Since, by definition, an advocate pleads, defends, and maintains the cause of another, Jesus stands ready to intercede for you so that you can speak with confidence in the Father's presence.

19

Jesus has provided us with backstage passes—full access to God, the Producer of eternity's greatest drama.

The writer of Hebrews also said:

Let us cling to him and never stop trusting him. [He] understands our weaknesses, for he faced all of the same temptations we do, yet he did not sin. So let us come boldly to the throne of our gracious God. There we will receive his mercy, and we will find grace to help us when we need it (Hebrews 4:14–16 NLT).

Jesus became the Advocate so you can take hold of the privilege of prayer with a confident faith, trusting that the Almighty Father is *your* Father, believing that He wants to hear about everything you hold in your heart.

In light of these Scriptures, you might consider your role in the life of your children as similar to that of Jesus—as an advocate and intercessory partner in prayer.

An Intercessory Calling. Since you have such an Advocate—Jesus—who has paved the way for you to enter the presence of God, why not become an advocate yourself? Why not see yourself as the one who holds open the door of prayer through which your children might enter.

The apostle Peter wrote:

You are a kingdom of priests, God's holy nation, his very own possession. This is so you can show others the goodness of God, for he called you out of the darkness into his wonderful light (1 Peter 2:9 NLT).

Every believer has received the call to be an intercessor as he relates to others around him, leading people to become intimately acquainted with Jesus. Considering that as the calling you have received, how could it ever have greater implications than when applied to your children? You can demonstrate the goodness of God by allowing them to be involved in your relationship with God, particularly when it comes to prayer.

Ask yourself:

★ **Is my faith in God obvious in the way that I pray?**

★ **Do my children see a confident joy in me as the result of prayer?**

An Intercessor's Confidence. Priests served as the "official" human advocates under the Jewish system. They were made holy by offering up sacrifices for their own sins before they began interceding on behalf of the people.

Our High Priest offered himself to God as one sacrifice for sins, good for all time. . . . And so, dear brothers and sisters, we can boldly enter heaven's Most Holy Place because of the blood of Jesus (Hebrews 10:12, 19 NLT).

The blood of Jesus qualifies you to pray "priestly" prayers on behalf of your children.

21

As a parent, all you have to do is call upon Jesus' sacrifice as your right of entry, and your way is clear to begin your intercessory prayer for your children's sake—pleading favor for your beloved offspring with powerful expressions of love and commitment.

The confidence to which you are entitled is based on the similarity between your love for each of your children and God's love for His Son—Jesus. He understands every nuance of your heart, every hopeful aspiration, every wistful longing, every ounce of anxiety,

In His life, Christ is an example, showing us how to live.

In His death, He is a sacrifice, satisfying for our sins.

In His resurrection, He is a conqueror.

In His ascension, He is a king.

In His intercession, He is a high priest.
—**Martin Luther**

and every glimmer of joy. You have a strong affinity with the Almighty in your bond as a parent, and you will find in Him a Father who understands, encourages, and answers lavishly.

God puts His ear so closely down to your lips that He can hear your faintest whisper.

Your confident intercession will lead you to pray boldly and unreservedly for your children, helping them to realize their worth in the eyes of God; helping them to learn to trust you and their heavenly Father for wise counsel and direction.

Ask yourself:

★ **Do my children sense my confidence in the Lord?**

★ **Do they know how much I pray for them?**

An Intercessor's Commitment. Peter continued his directive with these words.

Dear brothers and sisters . . . I warn you to keep away from evil desires because they fight against your very souls (1 Peter 2:11 NLT).

And the writer of Hebrews finished with these words:

Without wavering, let us hold tightly to the hope we say we have, for God can be trusted to keep his promise. Think of ways to encourage one another to outbursts of love and good deeds (Hebrews 10:23–24 NLT).

Your commitment as an advocate on your children's behalf is two-sided.

The Issue of Integrity

You must maintain high standards in pursuing God's will and a pure heart in relationship with other people. You cannot be effective in intercessory prayer if you are negligent of God's priorities in other areas of your life. It is the prayers of *righteous* men and women who move the heart of God to respond.

The Issue of Following Through

You must be devoted to training your children to be actively involved in loving others and committing outrageous deeds of goodwill. Your prayers should regularly include requests on behalf of people who need your love and good deeds. You will thereby teach your children what is the true role and responsibility of an intercessor.

Ask yourself:

★ **Do my children see me avoiding evil and actively pursuing holiness?**

★ **Do they hear me pray for others?**

★ **Do they see in me a willingness to be part of the answer to those intercessory prayers?**

**The prayer of a righteous man is
powerful and effective.**

JAMES 5:16

Since Jesus has shown you, by His example, how to be an advocate, why not get on with the business at hand? You have the privilege of prayer . . . at your immediate disposal.

23

Up Close and Personal

Once upon a time, a powerful emperor, returning from a fierce battle, marched triumphantly through the great city of Rome in order to display the evidence of his mighty conquest before his subjects. Following proudly behind, his soldiers marched in impressive array; and finally, the captives of war and the treasure-booty of victory were all paraded before the people.

The crowds cheered, throwing their caps into the air, tossing flowers and wreaths toward the emperor, clapping and bowing as he passed, shouting, "Long live the emperor!" Just as the pageant passed in front of the platform where the empress was seated, a little boy broke from his mother, pushed his way through the crowd, and ran boldly out into the street. Lunging forward, he grasped for the emperor's stirrup, intending to get a leg up and into his saddle. A soldier was quick to respond. He swept the little guy up into his arms to scold him and return him to his mother.

"Do you know who that is?" he chided, frowning at the boy. "He is the emperor!"

The boy hurried to explain: "You don't understand, he's my—" but before he could get the words out, the emperor's hand flew up into the air, bringing the parade to an abrupt halt. The clamor of the throng fell into an immediate hush. Everyone stood silently watching as the mighty warrior-king signaled to the legionary to come forward.

Thinking that he was about to be congratulated for his ready response, the legionary strutted into the emperor's presence.

"I may be *your* emperor," the great leader said, his brow furrowed in reproach as he reached to take the boy into his arms, "but I am *his* papa."

The most important thing you can teach your children in regard to prayer is that they are praying to their heavenly *Papa.*

That seems a little forward, you say? A little *too* familiar?

Unfortunately, modern Bible translations have interpreted the word "Abba" as "Father." In our vernacular, the term would be more appropriately translated "Daddy." It was the term used by Hebrew children to address their fathers. And though it was a title that indicated courtesy and respect, it was much more than that. The word "Abba" was used in the greater context of deep intimacy and complete trust.

> *Jesus referred to God as "Daddy"*
> *every other time He prayed.*

One of the reasons this is such an important point is that *every* record in the Gospels where you find Jesus praying or instructing His disciples concerning prayer, the word "Abba" is used in address to God, with the one exception uttered from the cross: "My God, my God, why have you abandoned me?" (Mark 15:34; Matthew 27:46 MSG). In other words, Jesus referred to God as "Daddy" every other time He prayed.

25

This is no trifling issue since Jesus had no precedent for using this intimate expression in His address to the Almighty. He was *establishing* a precedent and intentionally taught His disciples to follow His lead. So Jesus' use of the word "Abba" was a reflection of His *experience* of God, rather than His religious orientation.

In Matthew 6:9 NCV, it is recorded that Jesus said, *"Pray like this: 'Our Father [Abba, Daddy] in heaven, may your name always be kept holy.'"*

Jesus didn't consider this common term disrespectful or too familiar. In fact, He indicated that it exalts the name of God. It is the same as saying, "Our Daddy, enthroned in the heavens, we exalt you because you are worthy of our love and trust." In fact, He takes the time to illustrate that man's dependency upon God's faithfulness glorifies Him and pleases Him.

From God's perspective, praying to Him as Father endears Him to you. It echoes in His eternal ears in strains reminiscent of His beloved Son, Jesus.

> **This is what the LORD says: . . . I will comfort you as a mother comforts her child.**
>
> ISAIAH 66:12-13 NCV

Unfortunately, not all children have a pleasant and affectionate relationship with their fathers. The word *daddy* doesn't conjure up the same images in every youngster's mind; it varies from child to child. Fathers run the gamut from indifferent, harsh, and abusive to warm, fun, and tenderhearted. Your children's understanding of the heavenly Father will be directly affected by their earthly father's disposition and behavior.

The good news is, children have an opportunity to learn the true intent of fatherhood from the Almighty Abba. The apostle Paul said that the relationship believers have with God is not one of slavery, involving fear and punishment, but one of childlike trust that involves affectionate warmth and parental approval. (See Galatians 4:1-7.)

That was Jesus' experience with His Father. The extent to which Jesus adored His divine Daddy becomes evident in how frequently He stole away from people to be alone with Him, and how long He spent speaking with Him in prayer. He didn't dare make a move without consulting His *Abba*.

In John 5:19–20, the religious leaders of Jesus' day were outraged and astonished with Him because He had broken one of their cherished traditions by working a miracle of healing on a holy day. In a very straightforward manner, Jesus explained to them that He was doing exactly what His Father had shown Him to do.

Consider this scripture paraphrased:

"The truth is, I can do nothing by myself. I do only what I see Abba doing. Whatever Abba does, I do also. For Abba loves me and shows me everything He is doing. In fact, Abba will show me how to do even greater works than this. . . . Then you will truly be astonished."

These words of Jesus set a very good precedent for teaching children the essentials of prayer. Teach your children to:

★ **Speak to God as their Father, or, more importantly, as their heavenly Daddy.**

Impress upon your children's minds that God is tenderly watching over them in every aspect of their lives. Teach them that they can talk to Him about anything and everything on their hearts.

"Father God, I love you more than anything!"

★ **Submit to God as Father.**

Help your children understand how important it is that they show their respect for the Almighty by their thoughts, their words, their actions, and their plans for the future.

"Daddy in heaven, I want more than anything to please you!"

★ **Look for evidence of the Father at work.**

Beginning with nature hikes, going on to observations concerning people's lives, and finally even examining the struggles within their own hearts, teach your children to recognize God's hand at work in the world in which they live.

"Abba, I see your hand at work everywhere!"

★ **Join the Almighty Abba wherever you find Him working.**

Train your children to respond to every challenge as an opportunity to join God in His work. When someone is in need of mercy, when someone is feeling sad, when someone expresses an interest in spiritual matters, and even when a little sparrow falls out of his nest—all of these are opportunities for your children to put their hands in God's hands and help get the job done!

"Father God, I just want to be like you!"

★ Acknowledge that the Father loves them.

Help your children discover the evidence of God's love in their lives. Not simply the blessings of relationships and daily provisions, but the blessing of intelligence, health, curiosity, laughter, hard work, good memories, and even the blessings in failure.

> Prayer is weakness leaning on omnipotence.
> **–W. S. Bowden**

"Daddy in heaven, I see your love in every part of my life!"

★ Expect the Father to respond to them.

Impress upon your children the importance of anticipating and looking for God's response to them. Teach them to open their minds to the many ways the Father might answer their prayers. Get creative—He is!

"Abba, I can't wait to see what you say to this!"

★ **Expect the Father to do more than they expected Him to do.**

Help your children's faith to expand and make room for the generosity of God. He wants more for them than they want for themselves!

"Father God, surprise me!"

★ **Expect that their intimacy with the Father will blow people's minds.**

Train your children to be bold in prayer—asking the Father for lavish blessings on others. When the Lord answers those prayers, your children will have opportunity to witness to the love and faithfulness of the Almighty Abba.

"Daddy in heaven,
let's let some other people
in on the family secret!"

Nothing will energize and nurture your children's prayer lives as much as learning the truth about God as their divine *Daddy*.

Keep It Simple

**They think they will be heard
because of their many words.**

MATTHEW 6:7

Good communication isn't dependent upon how many words you say, nor upon how impressively you say them. Good communication is a very simple matter of speaking effectively. The key is, keep it simple.

Children have a natural advantage in communication. The younger they are the more straightforward they seem to be. They say whatever is on their minds without "beating around the bush." The reasons are obvious: They have a tendency to focus on the present, and they have a limited vocabulary. You can use the natural advantage that your children have to teach them a simple and powerful habit that works with any type of communication—especially prayer.

*Do not make prayer a monologue—
make it a conversation.*

Listen First and Listen Well. Prayer is two-way communication, not a monologue presented on an earthly platform for a heavenly audience. Many adults pray as if they are offering up a long list of petitions, interspersed with an occasional expression of praise guaranteed to convince God that they are neither unappreciative for past favors nor greedy about asking for more.

31

It is rare to hear someone pray in such a way that allows God an opportunity to say anything. No one would consciously advocate a completely self-centered method of communication in reference to another human being, yet many practice that protocol in prayer. Why not begin your prayer with a word from God—a verse of Scripture from the Psalms, from the Sermon on the Mount, or from the mouth of the Old Testament prophets. In other words, let God have the first word.

A very wise man named Solomon once said these words:

As you enter the house of God, keep your ears open and your mouth shut! Don't be a fool who doesn't realize that mindless offerings to God are evil. . . . So let your words be few. . . . Being a fool makes you a blabber-mouth (Ecclesiastes 5:1–3 NLT).

You have an opportunity to teach your children the profoundly conversant truth about prayer when you teach them to reflect on Scripture as a place to begin in prayer.

Say What You Mean and Mean What You Say. The reciprocity of conversational prayer allows your children an opportunity to speak to God about their personal, private concerns. Since the Almighty is their *Father* in heaven, it is important that they learn to talk to Him about anything and everything that is on their hearts or on their minds.

A child's whole existence will benefit from being taught that he can tell the Lord anything on his heart with the very expressions with which he feels it. Train your children to resist the temptation to fix their feelings with *nice sounding* words. God isn't fooled or impressed with people's attempts to "spiritualize" their feelings or motives—using stained-glass tones and expressions instead of honest words from an honest heart. God can handle anything that your children need to say. He simply wants them to trust Him enough to say it to Him.

An important aspect of this training comes with teaching your children that they don't have to explain everything they say. Because God possesses a superior knowledge of His people, He already knows how we feel and what we need. Impress upon your children that God simply loves to interact with them. He loves the sound of their voices, the expressions on their faces, and the way they express their love to Him.

Lead your children to the understanding that they can speak directly and to the point in prayer. The most important thing is meaning what you say.

Suggest that your children form an image in their minds regarding these conversations with God. They might sit in a chair that faces an empty chair. Or they might kneel before something they can picture as the throne of God. Perhaps your children would prefer to curl up in a big chair, imagining themselves crawling up into the lap of God, into His very arms, as they speak to Him.

Practice the habit of reciprocal, conversational prayer with your children along these lines:

Speak: "Our Father in heaven. . . ."

Listen: as God hushes the halls of heaven in response to your petition.

Speak: "May we honor your name, advance your kingdom, and do your will here on the earth where we live, just as the angels honor your name, tend to your kingdom, and accomplish your will in the heavenly realms."

Listen: as your heart considers reasons to honor God's name and ways to accomplish His will. Allow the Spirit of the Lord to move upon your heart concerning how that should be done. Teach your children not to strain after high and lofty thoughts, but simply to focus on letting the impulse of the Spirit speak through the silence. Be prepared that the Lord might bring up an idea or two.

> Prayer requires more of the heart than of the tongue.
> –Adam Clarke

Speak: Give verbal expression to aspects of your life and the lives of your children where God's honor and God's will need to be considered. It might be in relationships where there are struggles or temptations, or perhaps in areas of conduct or discipline, or even in insight and understanding. It could be issues of health, or decisions that are pending where God's wisdom and guidance are needed in order to ensure that His will is the priority.

Listen: for God's affirmation and encouragement in response. Be still and know that He has heard and has taken into account everything you have said.

Speak: "We trust that you know what we need—our daily provisions, our immediate needs, our concerns about the future." Teach your children to express their needs in a direct manner, yet without using a demanding tone.

Listen: to God's assurance. You might read a Psalm from the Bible that affirms the tender care God exercises over you.

Speak: "Please forgive us our sins and help us to be forgiving toward others." Your children will learn the healing and cleansing practice of confession as you lead them to express their weaknesses, their failings, and the darkness in their hearts. They will also learn to practice forgiveness as they ask a blessing upon the names of those who have hurt them, offended them, or mistreated them in any way.

Listen: to God's grace and forgiveness. In the stillness, practice hearing the quiet gentleness of God's love. Consider the atoning work of Jesus—the suffering at Calvary, the silence of the tomb, the glory of the resurrection—all affirming that forgiveness has been made available for those who trust Him for it. Likewise, God's grace is held out through those who have experienced it. Your children's ability to forgive will draw people to Jesus, as well.

Speak: "Don't let us give in to temptation, but deliver us from the evil one." Name the temptations, one by one. Practice the habit of giving Satan credit for the evil in the world so that your children will recognize the difference in God's goodness and the devil's darkness. There needs to be a strong impression of the contrast between good and evil in a world where there is so much gray.

Listen: for God's counsel and wisdom concerning the temptations you and your children are facing. Let Him convict you about ways to avoid evil and ways to embrace good.

Three-way conversations between you, your child, and your Father in heaven will be some of the greatest blessings in your own spiritual growth; but more, they will etch themselves upon your children's hearts like living words on a solid gold ingot.

For the Love of It

The young minister was new to the large parish and unfamiliar with the routine of his parishioners. Having been reared in a small town with a devout constituency, Pastor Jim had never been exposed to any extraneous, unreligious use of a church building; it had been used only by the public for Sunday worship, midweek prayer meetings, weddings, and funerals. Other than that, and only on dire occasions, people visited the premises individually, and specifically for the purpose of prayer.

Now in the big city, ascending the steps to the side door closest to his private study, Pastor Jim met two women of his congregation coming out. It just so happened that he had taken notice of this mother-daughter duo in services yesterday, as they seemed particularly distracted during his sermon. And if his discernment was worth anything, he would say their distraction was not of a spiritual nature.

The women's foreheads were beaded with sweat, and they each had a small towel dangling around their neck. These factors caused Pastor Jim to jump to some hasty—though impressive—conclusions.

"What is going on?" the minister asked, his brow furrowed with concern. He couldn't imagine what mother—particularly *this* mother—would have her daughter up so early in the morning, laboring so diligently in prayer that they came away bathed in sweat.

"Oh, nothing. We're here early every Monday morning," the older woman responded. "We've been in this habit for years."

"Really?" he said as his eyes widened with surprise.

"Yes, Brother Jim," she answered. "Does that shock you?"

"Well, yes . . . I just had a different impression of the two of you, that's all," he stammered apologetically. "May I commend you, dear Mother, for instilling this committed exercise into your daughter's habit? Furthermore, may I ask which room you occupy each week so that I might pray a blessing over it today?"

The two women exchanged a puzzled glance. The younger one answered, "The room across the hall from the library."

"Have a blessed day." Pastor Jim smiled, shaking each of their hands with both of his.

"You too," they said as they smiled, still a little taken aback.

Heading straight for the door that stood facing the library, and shaking his head in shame for having jumped to such ignoble conclusions about the two women, Jim put his hand on the knob. Reverently and slowly he turned the handle so as not to disturb the hallowed place. To his dismay, he found that the furnishings in the room consisted of—not a kneeling bench and an altar—a bench press and a treadmill.

Unfortunately, many parents teach their children a whole lot more about their habits of physical care and concern than they do about habitually tending to their spiritual growth and well-being.

> *Failure to establish good spiritual habits will lead to poor spiritual health.*

The Scriptures are full of encouragement about the habit of spontaneous prayer. People learn all kinds of habits, but too few practice the habit of prayer on an impulse.

★ A car in front of you starts hydroplaning, sliding across the median and into oncoming traffic. Is your first impulse one of prayer?

★ Your child awakens with a fever and a headache. Do you pray with her before phoning the doctor?

★ Your neighbor spreads an unkind rumor about your son's behavior at school. Do you pray for her before you launch your defense?

★ You receive a sizeable check in the mail from your husband's former employer, stating that an error had been detected in calculating his bonus from the previous year. Do you kneel to express thanks before loading the kids up to head to the mall?

> There are moments when whatever be the attitude of the body, the soul is on its knees.
> –Victor Hugo

Children learn more from your spontaneous reactions than from any of the well-planned words you speak. Develop the habit of prayer, and teach your children the joy of spontaneously speaking to God.

39

The habit of prayer when planning and prioritizing. Pray for and with your children as you schedule your day's activities, your priorities, and your special events. Jesus said that those who seek the kingdom of God as a first priority will be blessed in what they do. (See Matthew 6:33.) Train your children to develop the good habit of committing their top priorities to God's will. Listening to the will of the Lord, you will discover more time for serving others.

The habit of seeking help. Frequently, you find yourself in a crisis. It may be related to health, finances, relationships, time constraints, or any number of other issues. Children have the opportunity to learn more about true faith in these situations than in most others. Imitating your reactions to life's stresses and crises, they learn to lean upon the Lord—or to ignore Him altogether.

Train yourself in the habit of turning to the Lord as your first impulse in times of great need.

Each day is a gift to be opened with prayer.

The habit of giving thanks. What better habit than that of spontaneous gratitude offered to the Giver of all good gifts? Every day provides opportunity to thank God for a multitude of blessings. Develop the routine practice of expressing appreciation every morning and evening in the presence of your children, and you'll witness the nurturing of a grateful heart.

The habit of asking advice. When challenges confront you and your children, or when decisions are pending, the habit of seeking counsel from the Lord is one that will result in spontaneous blessing, as well. God's wisdom is generously provided when sought. Train your children—by your own conviction—to seek the Almighty when in need of good advice.

The habits of the heart. Spontaneous prayer becomes a habit lodged within the heart. It is a first noble impulse derived from the exercise of diligent faith. This kind of prayer habit will result in great joy and blessing—for your children, yourself, and your God!

41

> *Perfect prayer is that in which he who is praying is unaware that he is praying at all.*

Be joyful always; pray continually; give thanks in all circumstances, for this is God's will for you in Christ Jesus.

1 THESSALONIANS 5:16–18

Form and Substance

While the habit of spontaneous prayer nurtures your children's relationship with God, practicing the habit of structured prayer builds a much-needed spiritual discipline into their lives. Jesus exercised both types of prayer—spontaneous outbursts of expression and the daily discipline of intentional prayer. The point is, each serves a different purpose and produces a unique result. The one trains your children's impulses in heavenly channels, the other guides your children's thoughts, energy, and pursuits into God's priorities. Neither practice should preclude or exclude the other.

Free-flowing expressions of prayer usually stem from emotional reactions to immediate circumstances and stimuli: gratitude for blessings, cries for help, requests for wisdom. Wise parents help their children direct those reactions heavenward. But the disciplined times of prayer allow your children to go deeper than the immediate circumstances will provide. Structured times of prayer supply you and your children the opportunity to pursue God's interests as well as the needs of your family and other people.

Here are five suggestions for developing the discipline of prayer:

Sweet Hour of Prayer. The best guarantee for making prayer a daily discipline is to set aside an appointment for prayer—then keep it! Just as you would schedule an appointment at work, your child's medical checkup, or a gymnastics class, you need to teach your children the blessing of disciplined prayer by planning for regular times of prayer. The immediate benefit of a regular time of prayer promotes growth in relationship with God. The long-range benefit includes the subconscious prompting from somewhere deep inside—the still, small voice, whispering, "Keep your commitment to pray."

Holy Ground. Just as important as scheduling a time for prayer, the place of prayer is critical. It can become a very special altar in your children's experience. It would be wise to have your children help you pick out a special place in your home to which you can retreat for prayer. It may be a place conducive to kneeling, or occupying two chairs for sitting, or boasting a window before which to stand, or even furnished with a big fluffy rug where all of you can recline in prayer. Whatever place you choose, make certain that it is comfortable, clean, and appealing to your children. You will discover that it will become a hallowed place in your home—a very sacred place where you and your children regularly meet and talk with the Almighty.

> Christian character grows in the secret place of prayer.
>
> –Samuel M. Zwemer

Alone in the Garden. Solitude is critical in establishing an effective prayer time for you and your children. While making your selection of a time and a place for prayer, make sure that you will be uninterrupted and free from distractions. Your place of prayer should be free of ringing telephones, chattering televisions, audible computer notifications (such as "You've got mail"), or radio clutter. Quiet background music or fans can be effective in helping to block out other noises while providing a gentle atmosphere in which one's spirit might thrive. It is difficult to listen to God when all the worldly noise is barging in.

Be Still and Know. Teach your children to make preparation for prayer by taking the time to calm their minds and quiet their thoughts before beginning. Kneeling in the silence or reading a Psalm from the Scriptures will help all of you muzzle the clamor of life's busyness and activity, allowing you to center your thoughts upon God. You can help your children learn to shut their eyes and their mouths while opening their hearts to receive their heavenly Host.

Pray Like This. One day Jesus was teaching His followers some of the most important spiritual principles of all. Right in the middle of that inspirational and instructional discourse, He presented a very helpful format for prayer. (See Matthew 6:9–13.) Jesus taught His disciples a formula for prayer that will help you to keep your priorities in proper and powerful perspective:

★ **God as "Father."** Train your children to develop the habit of thinking of God as their heavenly Father. Essentially, they are speaking to their Divine Daddy. He is not distant, He is not distracted, neither is He disinterested. Help your children to realize that when they keep their scheduled commitment to prayer, God is waiting at the meeting place, anticipating their arrival before they ever show up. They are the apple of His eye, and He is always available to listen to them. And though He is admittedly the King of the big, wide universe, He is no less the King of their own, individual hearts.

★ **Celestial Concerns.** Help your children develop the habit of exploring in prayer how they may take part in honoring God's name, in advancing God's kingdom, and in accomplishing God's will. The emphasis on Jesus' words in this portion of "the Lord's Prayer" has earthly priorities mirroring the priorities in heaven. Very few people would dare to measure their own pursuits against those in celestial realms.

★ **Earthly Essentials.** Jesus progressed from those loftier matters to the more terrestrial issues: the need for daily bread, for forgiveness of sin, and for dealing with the pitfalls of human weakness—temptations and evil. Your children will learn to distinguish between "need" and "greed" when petitioning their heavenly parent as they see fit. They will learn the vital and therapeutic benefit of confession, the humbling experience of asking for mercy, and the ultimate expression of God's love in terms of forgiving others. And not least of all, your children will discover their greatest resource in dealing with the temptation to sin, by asking for help, for discernment, and for strength in the face of evil.

★ **"Aweful" Assignments.** Finally, teach your children to hold their heavenly Father in proper esteem—in holy awe—helping them to continue to grow in their faith. Acknowledging His sovereign right to exercise His will, His limitless power to meet their every need, and His radiant glory in everything He does will result in a growing awareness of God in their everyday existence.

*A habit of prayer is
one of the surest marks
of a true Christian.*

The habit of intentional prayer cannot be overemphasized. It is essential to your children's future success and happiness. So teach them that true prayer is a way of life, not just something you do when you're in trouble. Your children's spiritual well-being, relational stability, moral fiber, and emerging faith are dependent upon it.

46

Taking the Land

"Mama!" three-year-old Jesse yelled from his bedroom doorway. "Where's Jesse's lifesaver? There's a monster in here!"

"Do you mean your light saber?" his mother giggled to herself.

"Yeah!" he called back. "Jesse needs to fight!"

No doubt, one of the most challenging things about being a parent is teaching your children how to fight effectively in order to survive spiritually while living in a fallen world. Your children will face many types and varieties of moral dilemmas, threats to their safety and health, psychological upsets, emotional upheavals, relational difficulties, and the challenge of merely maintaining their integrity and sanity in the daily routine of living.

Because the struggles of living in this world are so prevalent upon young people, your responsibility to teach your children an effective strategy for spiritual warfare becomes pressing, as well. Every day presents to your children some kind of spiritual battle.

Contemporary cultural resources offer popular strategies and various medicinal remedies for dealing with depression, trauma, sleeplessness, separation, and loss; as well as for managing anger, grief, anxiety, and chemical and psychological addictions.

However, about two thousand years ago, the apostle Paul offered profound words of wisdom that

47

tend to get lost in the onslaught of therapies and treatments for coping with, managing, and overcoming life's most pressing difficulties.

Listen to his counsel.

Though we live in the world, we do not wage war as the world does. The weapons we fight with are not the weapons of the world. On the contrary, they have divine power to demolish strongholds (2 Corinthians 10:3–4).

The weapons Paul refers to are not "old world" armory steeped in superstitions and magical incantations. This armory consists of proven and timeless tactics that are available to every believer in any situation at any given time. Teach your children how to implement Paul's strategy for spiritual warfare as he outlines it in the epistle to the Ephesians. (See 6:11–18.)

Get creative about using visual aids to help teach your children these very practical and powerful ways to fight the spiritual war that is raging.

★ **Put on the full armor of God so that you can take your stand against the devil's schemes.**

The first step is to simply take responsibility for the need to prepare yourself for battle. Talk to your children about the battle in which they are engaged. Be open and thorough about the spiritual dangers that lurk about them.

★ **Our struggle is not against flesh and blood, but against the rulers, against the authorities, against the powers of this dark world, and against the spiritual forces of evil in the heavenly realms.**

Second, teach your children how to identify the enemy—the true enemy—Satan. Give them examples of how Satan might disguise himself in an effort to manipulate or seduce them.

★ Stand firm then, with the belt of truth buckled around your waist.

Sometimes truth refers to biblical doctrine, but in this case, it most likely refers to principles and ethics. If you have a long scarf or a belt made of fabric that can wrap several times around your child's waist, you can demonstrate how, as part of the body armor, practicing truthfulness protects them from falling victim to Satan's darts that slip in from below his line of vision. Satan's deceptions slither like a snake in the grass, sneaking up on them when they aren't looking.

★ With the breastplate of righteousness in place.

Perhaps a vest could serve as a breastplate. Explain to your children that this piece of body armor falls securely into place when they have carefully maintained their relationship with Jesus. The area of greatest vulnerability—the heart—is covered by staying close to the Lord.

★ And with your feet fitted with the readiness that comes from the gospel of peace.

A soldier's shoes or boots are critical—representing a readiness to spring into action with the good news about Jesus. Let your children put on some old boots or shoes and tromp around in them proclaiming the good news: "Jesus is my champion!"

49

★ **In addition to all this, take up the shield of faith, with which you can extinguish all the flaming arrows of the evil one.**

If you have a large pot lid, or a trash can lid, you can allow your children to practice their defensive moves from behind their shields. Help them to understand that their convictions and belief in God protect them from the fiery arrows of doubt with which Satan will bombard them throughout their lives.

★ **Take the helmet of salvation.**

Encourage your children to put on a hat of some type—preferably a hard one. The head is the most vulnerable part of the body. Teach your children that their ability to think clearly, to keep a clear vision of God, to communicate effectively to others, and to listen carefully is dependent upon their trusting the Lord—their Deliverer, their Savior. Sound thinking is the result of being secure with God.

★ **The sword of the Spirit, which is the word of God.**

Choosing something long but harmless, of course, like a wand from your vacuum, or a feather duster, let your children practice wielding a sword as their only offensive weapon. All of the armor so far has been defensive, but the Word of God is an offensive weapon that puts the enemy to flight. Jesus used this strategy in the wilderness temptations at the beginning of His ministry. It is so powerful and so impenetrable that Satan has no weaponry that can overcome it.

★ **Pray in the Spirit on all occasions with all kinds of prayers and requests. With this in mind, be alert and always keep on praying for all the saints.**

Finally, with all of their armor in place, pray with your children about each of these strategies for spiritual warfare. Impress upon their hearts the importance of remembering who the Commander of the Army is. Your children will learn to seek the guidance, protection, and strength of the Almighty in times of distress.

The battle is real. The enemy is strong. But the victory has already been claimed in the One who overcame on behalf of your children long before they were ever conceived. Teach them to realize that they are guaranteed victory in the struggle if they will keep their eyes on Jesus, their ears open to His voice, and their hearts always obedient to His will.

51

Prayer: A Parent's Legacy

In her late twenties, Melinda felt that her fatigue was greater than the circumstances warranted. But then, how would she know? She had never given birth before. Maybe all new mothers are exhausted at this stage of the game. Yet two months had passed since her son was delivered, and she was growing concerned that she hadn't gained back her strength and stamina.

If only Mom were around . . . she thought to herself, pushing the grief down into her stomach where it simmered most of the time.

Melinda's mother had suffered a tragic and untimely death due to an automobile accident several weeks into Melinda's pregnancy. Having just begun the precious mother-daughter talks that relate to pregnancy, childbirth, and child-rearing, they hadn't touched on the infant, post-partum stage that Melinda was now experiencing along with her firstborn son.

She tilted her body against the back of the rocker, holding tiny Will at her breast. It was now two o'clock in the morning. Will was still getting up twice every night. *Maybe I can sleep while he's nursing,* she thought. He gulped and choked, causing her to instinctively tip her head back down. As she did, the strangest impulse flashed across her mind. It was a vivid memory to which she had clung without even realizing it.

Melinda had been eight years old when her youngest brother, Matt, was born. One night, having heard her mother tiptoe by her door, Melinda sneaked out of bed and spied on Matt and her mom as they stepped through their middle-of-the-night routine. It was beautiful to watch, and now also to recall! Cradling Melinda's baby brother in her arms, her mom had waited until he had nuzzled his way to contentment, her head tilted down over the infant in her arms, and then her lips began moving as hushed words fell fluently from them. At first, Melinda had thought she was whispering to the infant. But straining to hear, she discovered that her mom was praying: "Father, I know you have laid great plans for his life. Help his daddy and me to train him—gently and patiently—toward that end."

Tears sprung into Melinda's eyes. Her mom's wisdom was speaking even now. Though gone, she had left Melinda the most important lesson of her life— prayer. Sniffing back the tears, Melinda began her most noble task that very moment. She felt an unusual peace and strength as she poured her heart out to the Lord concerning her infant son and her role as his mother.

As a parent, you are leaving a legacy. You may not be aware of it; it may or may not be a noble legacy; but you are leaving one, nonetheless. Parents who are committed to prayer leave their children a strong heritage that will be with them all of their lives—a rock bed of strength, wisdom, and spiritual maturity.

There are three critical components you are passing on to your children when they witness a strong commitment to prayer as a priority in your daily walk. In 1 Corinthians 13:13 NLT, Paul referred to it this way:

**There are three things that will endure—
faith, hope, and love—
and the greatest of these is love.**

An enduring legacy of faith. You are the most profound influence in your children's lives. Though that places a great burden of responsibility on your shoulders, it also puts you in a position of great opportunity. That means that when it comes to faith, no one will impact your children's development in their relationship with the Lord like you will. Your children will grow to trust the Lord proportionate to your own trust in Him.

Prayer is a consistently prominent element in authentic faith. Faithful people are prayerful people. Many parents plan their times of prayer during their children's sleeping or school hours. Though it is sometimes essential to pray without interruption or distraction, it is also critical that your children witness you in the act of prayer.

Pray regularly with your children, giving full expression to your faith in God, and giving voice, as well, to your aspirations for each child's faith.

An enduring legacy of hope. On one unforgettable occasion, a young boy discovered his father kneeling at the bedside of his ailing brother. The boy knelt respectfully at his father's side, listening in on his prayer, adding his quiet "amen" from time to time. Tears streamed down the father's face and his voice broke intermittently with emotion.

Eventually, the young boy opened his eyes just a crack and peeked up at his brother lying under the blankets. His face held a frightening paleness, his eyes appeared sunken into his skull, and his lips were drawn tightly across his teeth. A clammy sweat beaded up on his brow, and the smell of infection filled the young boy's nostrils with a nauseating effect. In that moment, he realized that his sibling was much sicker than he had known—close to death.

His father's prayer continued for what seemed like hours. The young boy's legs began to tingle and grow numb. He shifted his weight to allow his blood to circulate better, laying his head against his father's elbow where it rested atop the bed. Eventually, the boy fell sound asleep.

Startled at the sound of a hearty "Amen!" the boy jerked awake. He looked up to see his father's face, radiant with an expression of hope.

"Father, how long have we been praying?"

"A little more than an hour."

"What took so long?"

"I had to pray through, son."

"Pray through what?"

"Pray through the fog of doubt and disbelief; pray through until I got a firm hold on my hope."

The prayer of genuine faith leaves a deep impression of hope within the heart of a child. Even when things do not turn out as wished, a child is left with the distinct impression of peace, knowing that there is a higher power—the Father of all who believe.

An enduring legacy of love. Love is never more faithful than when consumed in prayer. As a parent, you demonstrate your love for your sons and daughters by remaining faithful in prayer for their sake.

One day a seven-year-old named Lisa was with her mother at the grocery store. The two of them happened to see a little boy putting a candy bar into his coat pocket. Lisa's mother took notice of his disheveled appearance and approached the boy with kindness.

"Excuse me," she interrupted.

Startled, the boy said, "What ya want?"

"My daughter and I just happen to have an extra dollar on us today and wondered if you could use it to make a purchase?"

"Sure." The little guy blushed, holding out his hand.

"Good!" the young woman exclaimed, handing him the money.

The mother and daughter watched from a distance as the boy paid for the candy bar.

"Mama?" Lisa said as she looked up at her.

"What is it, Honey?"

"Why did you give him that dollar instead of giving him a scolding?"

"Because it looks to me like he might not have anyone praying for him," she explained, looking sad.

Love prays. And parents who love deeply pray a great deal.

Be aware that you are leaving a legacy for your children. Make it intentional. Make it a legacy of prayer. You cannot afford to pass up this amazing opportunity.

Hand in Hand, a Child and I

Dear Lord, I do not ask that Thou should give me
some high work of Thine,
Some noble calling or some wondrous task;
Give me a little hand to hold in mine;
Give me a little child to point the way
Over the strange sweet path that leads
to Thee;
Give me a little voice to teach to pray;

Give me two shining eyes Thy face to see.
The only crown I ask, dear Lord, to wear
Is this—that I may teach a little child.
I do not ask that I should ever stand
Among the wise, the worthy, or the great;
I only ask that softly, hand in hand,
A child and I may enter at Thy gate.

AUTHOR UNKNOWN

P-etition

R-everence

A-doration

Y-earning

E-xpectation

R-equests

Choosing a Holy Destination

Types of Prayer

I urge that supplications, prayers, intercessions, and thanksgivings be made for everyone, for kings and all who are in high positions, so that we may lead a quiet and peaceable life in all godliness and dignity.

1 TIMOTHY 2:1–2 NRSV

We human beings speak to each other in a variety of ways. Sometimes we are quite serious, discussing issues of critical importance; sometimes we just want to express our emotions—how much we love and care for one another. Still other times, our intention is to ask for a favor, forgive a wrong, offer a word of thanks, or compliment someone on a job well done. Our conversations can be at one time formal take-care-of-business talks and at other times light and carefree.

> More spiritual progress can be made in one short moment of speechless silence in the awesome presence of God than in years of mere study.
> –A. W. Tozer

Conversation with God—prayer—is no different. It takes many different shapes and forms. It can be serious and formal or endearing and lighthearted. The Bible mentions at least six different types of prayer or ways of communicating with God, all approved and encouraged. Let's take a look at these diverse expressions.

60

Prayers of Petition

Daniel . . . makes his petition three times a day.
DANIEL 6:13 NKJV

The word *petition* means to ask for something, but in a formal way according to law. We petition Congress for certain legislation. We petition the court for a ruling favorable to our cause. It is in essence a legal term.

The prayer of petition is intended to remind us of the legal standing we have before God because of Christ's death for us. We have been given access to His very throne. It is not because we are pitiable that God hears our petitions, but because we have been made fully acceptable in His sight.

> The reason we must ask God for things He already intends to give us is that He wants to teach us dependence, especially our need for himself.
> —**Erwin W. Lutzer**

Jesus Christ has made it possible for us to take every problem, every concern, every injustice to the court of God. There we are able to ask Him to review our grievances, hear our case, and render a just verdict. We need never sit back and accept as final what life throws at us. We are citizens of the kingdom of God in good standing. We are children of the King of kings. When presented, our petitions are heard.

When you bring your children before God in prayer, wage a legal battle in the courts of God. Submit and entrust your child to God's will, then stand your ground against the enemy, refusing to be intimidated.

61

Prayers of Reverence

*Let us . . . offer to God an acceptable worship
with reverence and awe.*

HEBREWS 12:28 NRSV

In any court of law, the jury has power, the lawyers have standing, and the defendant has rights—but the judge rules over all. The courtroom essentially belongs to him or her, and those who would bring their petitions to that court must acknowledge that and respect it.

> Some people pray just to pray and some people pray to know God.
> —Andrew Murray

We have been given standing in the courts of God. We have been given responsibility and rights as well, but our petitions will not be addressed unless we have a solemn reverence for the ultimate instrument of justice, the judge. This is important because we will not put our faith in the decision of the court if we do not reverence and respect the judge.

Prayers of reverence and respect are prayers that honor and proclaim God's greatness and power. They remind us not of who we are, but of who He is! They enable us to put our faith in His just rulings.

Take your children to God in prayer, and as you do, remember that you are not taking them to some low, impotent court. You are speaking on their behalf in the highest court in the land—indeed, in all of eternity.

Prayers of Adoration

My lips shall praise thee.
PSALM 63:3 KJV

Prayers of adoration include words of thankfulness, praise, worship, and devotion. These prayers serve to solidify our faith that the petitions we take before the court will be heard and fairly considered. As we speak words celebrating the Judge who holds our petition in His mighty hands, we reestablish our confidence in Him and the character of His courtroom. And giving thanks reminds us that God has been faithful to deal with us fairly in the past.

> Adoration is the highest form of prayer.
> –Louis Cassels

Our prayers are only as powerful, truthful, and good as the court in which they are presented. God runs an impeccable courtroom, and the entire process is lifted as we remind ourselves, our children, and even our enemies that our God reigns!

Prayers of Yearning

Blessed are those who hunger and thirst for righteousness.
MATTHEW 5:6

The prayer of yearning is a prayer that cries out to God. This is no hasty, dispassionate presentation. It tells God that we mean business. We are yearning for justice, for understanding, for wisdom. We hunger for it.

Teach your children to fill their prayers with yearning for God's best, His perfect will. Share with them the rewards of serving the Lord, of trusting in His fairness, mercy, and grace until they are longing for more and more of Him. Challenge them to take their deepest issues before Him, to taste and see that the Lord is good. (See Psalm 34:8.)

A yearning heart is one that is perpetually filled. It doesn't wait until the cup is empty to seek more of God. Go to His courtroom early and stay late. Yearn for His just decrees. Hold your children by the hand and take them with you into the throne room. There is no growth without yearning.

Prayers of Expectation

Elijah . . . prayed fervently that it might not rain.
JAMES 5:17 NRSV

Prayers of expectation loose the mind and the heart to receive the Judge's great and just decrees. Too often we limit God with our puny thinking. We believe that if we can't imagine it, it must be impossible. But nothing is impossible with God.

As you take hands with your children and walk into the courtroom to present your petitions, remind yourself—and them—that this is an opportunity with unlimited potential. Encourage them to look beyond their own trivial matters and reach out to change the world.

Prayers of expectation bridge the gap between what we can imagine and what God can do! They consist of words such as: "Use me, Lord, to accomplish your great purposes in the earth"; "Open my heart to receive knowledge and understanding beyond my years"; "Provide me with the resources to do mighty works in your name!" These are the prayers of expectation—the prayers that avail much.

> Beware in your prayers, above everything else, of limiting God . . . Expect unexpected things, "above all that we ask or think." Each time, before you intercede, be quiet first and worship God in His glory. Think of your place and privilege in Christ and expect great things!
> —**Andrew Murray**

65

Prayers of Request

Let your requests be made known to God.

PHILIPPIANS 4:6 NKJV

Ah yes, prayers of request. These are avenues through which we ask God for specific things. To these the mighty Judge may say yes or He may say no, depending on what is best for the specific individual and situation before Him. These prayers deal with those things that cannot so easily be identified as God's sovereign already knowable will.

And yet, the Judge urges us to take our requests before Him. He says that we have not because too often we ask not. He also says He delights in giving us good things.

Urge your children to take their requests before God and leave them there, humbly trusting Him to do what is best. These prayers teach humility and submission to God's will. They strip us of greed and selfishness, while teaching us that our Judge is also a loving Father who is anxious to keep us from the heartache and confusion that we often would bring on ourselves.

> It is a very good thing to ask. For if through conversing with a person of great power no small benefit is gained, what great benefit will one not gain from conversing with God? He is surely able to grant us our requests even before we ask Him; nevertheless He holds off and waits, so that we may have an occasion for being justly deserving of His providence.
>
> **–John Chrysostom**

66

Prayer is the simplest form of speech
That infant's lips can try;
Prayer the sublimest strains that reach
The Majesty on high.

O Thou by whom we come to God,
The Life, the Truth, the Way!
The path of prayer thyself hast trod;
Lord, teach us how to pray!

James Montgomery

What a spirit—what a confidence was in his very expression! With such a reverence he petitioned, as one begging of God, and yet with such hope and assurance, as if he spoke with a loving father or friend.

Someone Who Heard Martin Luther Praying

Flying High Overhead

Attitudes of Prayer

If my people, who are called by my name, will humble themselves and pray and seek my face and turn from their wicked ways, then will I hear from heaven and will forgive their sin and will heal their land.

2 CHRONICLES 7:14

Fervent

> That prayer has great power which a person makes
> with all his might. It makes a sour heart sweet, a
> sad heart merry, a poor heart rich, a foolish heart
> wise, a timid heart brave, a sick heart well, a blind
> heart full of sight, a cold heart ardent. It draws
> down the great God into the little heart; it drives
> the hungry soul up into the fullness of God; it
> brings together two lovers, God and the soul, in a
> wondrous place where they speak much of love.
>
> **Mechthild of Magheburg**

Fervent. When describing heat, it means very hot, white-hot. When describing prayer, the meaning is similar. It is prayer offered with great intensity, or white-hot zeal.

It's not a matter of working up emotions. In fact, a person praying this way may be quite calm. The intense feelings come naturally when you are confronted with a crisis, when someone you care deeply about is in danger, when life and death issues are at stake, when it could mean the difference between heaven and hell for someone you love, when your soul experiences a longing or heartbreak too deep for words.

The human frame can't always handle such intense emotions, so it sometimes goes into shock or breaks down. But when you are a follower of Christ, you are no longer just an ordinary person. The Spirit of God Almighty lives in you, and you have His power at your disposal. All of that energy can and should be channeled into prayer. Like a laser concentrates light, fervent prayer concentrates God's power to move mountains and win spiritual battles against the forces of darkness. (See Mark 11:22–24; Ephesians 6:12; and Romans 8:26–28.)

What the *King James Version* of the Bible calls "fervent" prayer, the *Amplified Bible* describes as "earnest (heartfelt, continued)." It goes on to say that this type of prayer "makes tremendous power available [dynamic in its working]" (James 5:16). Elijah's fervent prayer ended a three-and-a-half-year drought (vv. 17–18).

When the situation warrants and you feel the tide of fervent prayer rising, don't hold back. Pray intensely, using God's promises as your sword (Hebrews 4:12), and teach your children to do the same. Your prayers will avail much.

**The effectual fervent prayer of a
righteous man availeth much.**

JAMES 5:16 KJV

71

Heartfelt

Prayer is a sincere, sensible, affectionate pouring out of the soul to God, through Christ in the strength and assistance of the Spirit, for such things as God has promised.

John Bunyan

A heartfelt prayer is a sincere one, flowing from a heart of genuine concern. Paul's prayers in the Bible provide excellent examples. His interest in the well-being and spiritual growth of those he served was a result of the meaningful relationship that he had with them. These weren't strangers he was praying for. He *knew* these people and cared for them deeply. To convey his sincere love, he even wrote, "I have you in my heart."

Prayer is not eloquence, but earnestness.
–Hannah More

Likewise, you have people in your heart—family and friends you care for deeply. You want them to experience every blessing that God has provided for them. Let this heartfelt desire draw you into prayer, for when you pray, *things happen.*

But how do you get started? What do you say? The heavenly Father knew we would need help, so He included many examples in His Word. You are probably familiar with the Lord's Prayer in Matthew 6:9–13, where Jesus taught His disciples to pray. In the Psalms, David's prayers are certainly heartfelt as he pours out his soul. And Paul's prayers that are mentioned above are found in Ephesians 1:17–19; 3:16–21; Philippians 1:9–11; Colossians 1:9–12; and 2 Thessalonians 1:11–12. Try reading these in different Bible translations to see which one most mirrors what is in your heart.

Try writing out these prayers on index cards, inserting the names of the people you are praying for. By doing this, your children can follow along and pray with you. Another benefit is the confidence that you are praying scripturally—and those prayers always get results!

> **My deep feeling for you all comes from the heart of Christ Jesus himself.**
>
> **PHILIPPIANS 1:8 TEV**

Humility

> Humility is not a mere insulated grace like
> patience, or meekness, or any other virtue, but
> a feeling which pervades the whole man, and
> is called forth into exercise with every grace.
>
> **Charles Simeon**

Grace and humility are closely linked elements of a fruitful prayer life, yet humility is something we humans find difficult to achieve. We pride ourselves on being independent and self-sufficient. We want to be in charge and have our own way. Our flesh cringes at the thought of being dependent on anyone, yet that is the very thing God wants from us. Humble dependence upon Him is to be at the heart of our relationship.

So what does it mean to be humble?

★ **Humility recognizes that you are a finite being, limited in your ability, but nothing is impossible with God.**

★ **Humility takes God at His Word, even when all hope appears lost.**

★ **Humility admits weaknesses but looks to God's grace for strength.**

★ **Humility acknowledges that when you and God don't agree, He is right.**

★ **Humility graciously accepts all of the good that God offers.**

★ **Humility understands that there is nothing you could ever do to make yourself worthy enough to have your prayers answered. But it receives the gift of God's grace—His unmerited favor—with eternal gratitude.**

★ **Humility recognizes that Almighty God loves you enough to listen to your requests and grant those that are according to His will (His Word).**

★ **Humility acknowledges that without God there would be no answered prayer.**

★ **Humility is a choice.**

Jesus said that we must humble ourselves like a little child in order to inherit His kingdom. Perhaps rather than trying to teach this lesson to your kids, it is one you can learn from them.

> **"God opposes the proud**
> **but gives grace to the humble."**
> **Submit yourselves, then, to God.**
> **Resist the devil, and he will flee from you.**
>
> JAMES 4:6–7

75

Patience

It is not enough for the believer to begin to pray, nor to pray correctly; nor is it enough to continue for a time to pray. We must patiently, believingly continue in prayer until we obtain an answer. Further, we have not only to continue in prayer until the end, but we have also to believe that God does hear us and will answer our prayers. Most frequently we fail in not continuing in prayer until the blessing is obtained, and in not expecting the blessing.

George Müller

Have you ever heard the prayer, "Lord, give me patience, and give it to me now"? In our fast-paced society—with nearly everything available "on demand"—waiting patiently is not something we are accustomed to. Yet this fruit of the Spirit has always been a virtue for those seeking to walk in God's ways.

In order to receive answered prayer, several things are necessary. First, you must be God's child, born again into the family of God. Then you must make sure that your request agrees with the promises and principles in His Word. Next, you present your prayer to God in Jesus' name. Then you receive your answer by faith. The next one is the biggie—you must patiently wait for the answer to materialize.

Do you remember as a child when your parents promised that you were going to do something special like go on vacation? You were so excited you could hardly stand it. You never doubted that what they said would come to pass, but there was a time gap between their promise and the actual event. They probably said, "Be patient. The time will come." Patience is what carries you from point A to point B.

So how do you develop patience? The primary thing is to keep promises before you. Read them, recite them, meditate on them. As your body needs food for fuel, faith and patience need

> Patience means waiting without anxiety.
> –St. Francis of Sales

God's Word. The more you feed on it, the stronger you become and the more endurance you develop. Patience gives you that "peace that passes understanding" so that you can rest confidently, knowing that what God promised, He will bring to pass.

Imitate those who through faith and patience inherit the promises.

HEBREWS 6:12 NKJV

77

Joy

> For me, prayer is a surge of the heart;
> it is a simple look turned toward heaven,
> it is a cry of recognition and of love,
> embracing both trial and joy.
>
> **Thérèse of Lisieux**

You know the joy that you experience when you finally receive something you really, really want? When a prayer is answered, joy is the natural result. But did you know that you can experience that same joy even *before* you see the fulfillment of your request? In fact, you should.

> The opposite of joy is not sorrow. It is unbelief.
> –Leslie Weatherhead

That's what faith is all about. Faith believes it receives the answer when it prays. Hebrews says that "faith is the *substance* of things hoped for, the *evidence* of things not seen" (11:1 NKJV, emphasis added). It is confident that what God has promised, He will bring to pass. Faith is so confident that it experiences joy as if the answer has already arrived. This is possible when you believe that what you *can't see* is every bit as real as what you *can see.* Joy comes naturally when you believe that what is in the spirit realm will manifest in the physical world.

When Jesus hung on the cross, He was able to endure the agony because of "the joy that was set before Him" (Hebrews 12:2 NKJV). The joy that was set before Him was the promise of the resurrection. Jesus had a

78

confident expectation that God would do what He said He would do. He saw the end result. Despite the physical pain and mental anguish, joy was present, and it carried Him through to victory.

When you pray with your children, always use Bible promises as the basis of your faith. Then begin to talk about the answer as an established fact. God will do what He said He will do, so rejoice!

Count it all joy when you fall into various trials.

JAMES 1:2 NKJV

Confidence

> Prayer is obtained to this end that we should confess our needs to God, and bare our hearts to Him as children lay their troubles in full confidence before their parents.
>
> **John Calvin**

Do you or your child have a request to present to God? Abraham in the Old Testament yearned for a son, and God promised to give him one. Sounds simple enough, right? But Abraham was nearly one hundred years old and Sarah was way past childbearing years. Impossible.

Amazingly, Abraham had an unshakeable confidence in God. The Bible says, "He did not consider his own body, already dead (since he was about a hundred years old), and the deadness of Sarah's womb. He did not waver at the promise of God through unbelief, but was strengthened in faith, giving glory to God, and being fully convinced that what He had promised He was also able to perform" (Romans 4:19–21 NKJV).

We learn some important principles about faith from Abraham.

1) He did not consider the negative circumstances.

2) He chose to believe God's promise unwaveringly, refusing doubt.

3) He gave God glory before the promise was fulfilled.

4) He was fully convinced—had total confidence—that God would honor His Word.

Believing is being confident without seeing.
–George Morgan

Confident prayer begins where the will of God is known. And the will of God is revealed in the Bible. In it, you and your children can find promises that relate to every conceivable situation you will ever face. It may take some digging to find these nuggets of truth, but the effort will be well worth it, for it will enable you to pray with confidence, knowing your heavenly Father will grant your request.

81

This is the confidence that we have in Him, that if we ask anything according to His will, He hears us. And if we know that He hears us, whatever we ask, we know that we have the petitions that we have asked of Him.

1 JOHN 5:14–15 NKJV

Openness

Tell God all that is in your heart, as one unloads
one's heart, its pleasures and its pains, to a dear
friend. Tell Him your troubles, that He may
comfort you; tell Him your joys, that He may sober
them; tell Him your longings, that He may purify
them; tell Him your dislikes, that He may help you
conquer them; talk to Him of your temptations
that He may shield you from them; show Him the
wounds of your heart, that He may heal them.

François Fénelon

"Get real." When someone says that, they are telling
you to drop any pretense and just tell it like it is. This type
of openness is necessary for any relationship to have
meaningful depth to it.

This is the type of relationship that God wants us to
have with Him. He's given us an open door to His throne
room—which is amazing in itself—and we are free to
enter at any time and "let it all hang out."

In order for this type of communication to work
properly, certain things are required of each individual.
First, you must have the courage to be honest. Baring your
soul can be scary, unless you are confident that your
words won't be rejected or used against you.

That brings up God's part, and He has made it clear in
His Word that He will not condemn or reject you. When
you draw near to Him, He draws near to you. He'll never
force you to go deeper, but like a gentleman, He patiently

waits till you are ready to unfold the next layer of your concern. Then He holds your prayer in the strictest of confidence. He will never betray you. He will always validate your feelings and help you work through them. Then, when you are ready, He will gently guide you—or others—to bring about the resolution you seek.

> To pray "in Jesus' name" means to pray in his spirit, in his compassion, in his love.
>
> **–Kenneth L. Wilson**

Think of prayer as a heart-to-heart conversation between two soul mates. Open, honest, comforting, and healing. Create this type of safe environment for your children to be open with you. Then lead them to the throne room, where all of you can chat.

O my people, trust in him at all times.
Pour out your heart to him,
for God is our refuge.

PSALM 62:8 NLT

Compassion

Interviewer:
You love people whom others
regard as human debris.
What is your secret?

Mother Teresa:
My secret is simple.
I pray.

84

Compassion is a wonderful thing. More than deeply caring, it is love mixed with sorrow. But true compassion is far from passive. It moves you to do something to alleviate the suffering of another. The Bible says that Jesus was "*moved* with compassion" and healed the sick. (See Matthew 14:14 KJV.) Not only did their pain and suffering grieve Him, but compassion stirred Him to do something about it—He healed them.

An amazing attribute of compassion is that it can even turn enmity into affection (at least temporarily) if an enemy is in extreme distress. It was this type of compassion that led Jesus to petition His Father from the cross, saying, "Father, forgive them, for they know not what they do" (Luke 23:34 KJV). Their suffering wasn't apparent at the time, but Jesus knew the penalty that awaited His executioners unless they turned to God in repentance.

Certainly you've felt that tug at your heartstrings when you witness the plight of the forgotten ones in society. Maybe you've even felt it toward someone who has wronged you as you witnessed them reaping the seeds of devastation they sowed into your life.

The next time you feel the tug of compassion, pray. Through prayer you become God's conduit in the earth. You may or may not feel led to do something tangible, but even more important, your prayers rising up to heaven open the line for miracles to begin to flow to the object of your love. Teach this to your children and make your family a team of loving prayer warriors.

As God's chosen people, holy and dearly loved, clothe yourselves with compassion.

COLOSSIANS 3:12

85

Authority

Some years ago in China, at a meeting of missionaries and Chinese pastors, one of the Chinese pastors made a striking address. He said that he and his brethren were more than grateful to those who brought them the Word of life and the gospel of the Lord Jesus Christ, but yet, he said, there was one thing more which missionaries should teach their spiritual children. This new thing was to pray with authority, so that they might know how to take their stand in faith before the throne and rebuke the forces of evil, holding steady and firm, and gain the victory over them. That same need is tremendously evident today in the experiences of all that are seeking to walk closely with the Lord, and to stand for Him in the face of increasing opposition. Some have spoken of this as "throne prayer"—praying with one's hand touching the throne of God.

T. Stanley Sotau

One of the things that people marveled at when they observed Jesus was that He spoke with such authority. He rebuked storms and they ceased. He cast out devils with His Word. He knew His authority.

Once when Jesus entered Capernaum, a centurion approached Him, asking Him to help his servant who lay at home paralyzed and suffering terribly. Jesus immediately responded that He would go and heal the servant.

To that, the centurion replied, "Just say the word from where you are, and my servant will be healed! I know, because I am under the authority of my superior officers and I have authority over my soldiers. I only need to say, 'Go,' and they go" (Matthew 8:8–9 NLT).

This astonished Jesus, and He remarked that He had not found anyone in Israel with such great faith.

Today Jesus still works miracles through His words, only now they are spoken through His body of believers. He gave us authority to use His name and said that we would not only do the works that He did, but even greater works. When we pray in Jesus' name, it carries the same authority as if the words came from Jesus' very own lips. When we pray according to the Bible, this is literally true because the Bible is His Word.

Just as a minister has been given the authority to pronounce a couple husband and wife, you have been given authority to conduct kingdom business in the earth.

[Jesus said,] "I will do whatever you ask in my name, so that the Son may bring glory to the Father. You may ask me for anything in my name, and I will do it."

JOHN 14:13–14

To pray with understanding is to pray
as being instructed by the Spirit
in the understanding of the want of
those things which the soul is to pray for.

John Bunyan

Avoiding a Loss of Altitude

Pitfalls to Effective Prayer

**You ask and do not receive,
because you ask with wrong motive.**

JAMES 4:3 NASB

Once you've made the commitment to set some time aside each day to lead your children in the worshipful act of prayer, you may be wondering what, exactly, you should say. The responsibility of ushering your children into the throne room of almighty God can seem a little daunting at times. You want your prayers to be personal, yet you don't want to misguide your children with any of your words.

Maybe you've been unimpressed by prayers that seem insincere or showy. Perhaps you have some childhood memories of feeling like you were being lectured during family prayer time.

The best way to avoid some of the pitfalls that may keep you from freely entering into meaningful prayer time with your children is to recognize and acknowledge some of the common mistakes parents tend to make. Then you will be equipped with the confidence to enter into heartfelt conversations between you, your children, and your Creator.

Using Prayer to Further Your Purpose Rather Than God's

Parents want the best for their children. They want them to be happy and successful and eternally secure individuals, and that desire is God-given. It is the motivational key to keeping us on the job, giving our all for our kids.

> True life changing, problem solving, miracle-working prayer has one goal only— not our will, but God's.
> —Angela Garney

91

There is a stumbling block, however, that can leave us feeling frustrated and ineffective in our prayers for our kids. So much do we want good things for our children that we sometimes forget that God often defines "good" differently than we do.

It could be that God has a plan for your child that is a wide deviation from your own. Perhaps He has planned a path that includes financial hardship or service that carries with it no status or public acknowledgement. God may have a spouse for your child who is not a favorite of yours—someone He sees will further His purposes in your child's life.

Be diligent to seek God's perspective when praying for your kids. Ask Him to strip away your prejudices and selfish ambitions. Most of all, remember that God's highest purpose for your child is often the character derived from overcoming adversity. It will not always be a comfortable ride—for your child or for you—but it will pay grand, eternal rewards.

Using Prayer to Manipulate Your Children's Choices

When we pray with our children, it's a given that they are listening to our prayer even when it is being addressed to God. It is tempting to use this corporate prayer scenario to try to influence our children. This is a losing strategy. Not only does it pollute open communication between your child and God, but it turns prayer time into a lecture rather than a joint conversation with a kind and good heavenly Father.

> Beware of sublime prayers and of all the lies they make us tell.
> —Louis Evely

It's never a good idea to blur the line between what you as the parent want for your child and what God, your child's heavenly Father, wants. Avoid lateral prayers and keep your words directed to God. If you have something to say to your child, use another forum to say it.

As you and your children grow in regard to prayer, a relationship is being strengthened that will serve your children long after you are no longer in the picture. They will feel comfortable talking to God about issues in their lives and listening for His input.

Remember that in your prayers together your role is guide, friend of a friend, facilitator. You don't want to become God in your children's lives. No matter how good a parent you are or how noble your intentions, they deserve better.

Using Prayer As an Excuse for Living in Denial

We all have an image in our heads of the ideal family. Though it may vary wildly from person to person, still there is a tendency to try to make our families align with our fantasies—even in prayer.

The trouble is that unless we are being open and honest about who we are and what issues we are facing, we are living in denial and our prayers are wasted. God works only in the world of reality. He has no use for make-believe.

> I do not think that prayer saves us from having to face things that we do not want to face.
> –William Barclay

As you pray with your children, cast away the pretty platitudes and wishful thinking. Without falling into the trap at the other end of the spectrum—shock talk—take your case fairly and honestly to the Lord. Let your children see you admitting wrongdoing and calling things what they are—and urge them to do the same.

When you are willing to give up your image of the picture-perfect family, God is able to bring His image to bear on you and your kids' lives. No more facades and superficial nonsense; you can be real with each other and the world around you. What a relief!

Using Prayer to Avoid Responsibility

It's the old shell game. You don't want to confront someone—one of your kids for example—so you pray and ask God to do it for you. "Lord, please speak to _____. He never listens to me." "Lord, could you show _____ that what he's doing is wrong? If I tell him, he'll just get mad." God is always available to help us with our responsibilities, but He isn't going to do for us what He expects us to do for ourselves in our role as parents.

As a parent, there are issues you will need to address with your children. Those situations require face time and strong words from your mouth to your children's ears. No amount of prayer will convince God to usurp your role as a parent. What He will do is help you to find the right words to say, the right timing, the best possible strategy for dealing with issues. All you have to do is ask Him. His help is always available.

Prayer is a beautiful gift. Use it to ask God to do what only He can do in your children's lives.

Making God the "Fall Guy"

On any given day the job of a godly parent is tough as nails, requiring more than any reasonable person could possibly give. No one said it was easy, and maybe that's why we are often tempted to cut ourselves a break and let God take the fall.

Your child wants to go on an overseas mission trip, but you're reluctant to let him go. So many dangers. *How could God possibly be in this?* you wonder. Trouble is you know your child will be angry and disappointed if you say no simply on the basis of your personal fears and insecurities—so you bring God into it. "I prayed about it," you say, "and I feel like God is saying it's too dangerous and you should stay here." It's even possible to convince yourself that that's what God did say . . . or would have said.

Is prayer your steering wheel or your spare tire?

Being honest with your kids, taking the heat for parental decisions, takes courage. But you'll feel better when you do. Making God the bad guy will eventually backfire when your children decide that God really is a bad guy who wants to keep them from pursuing life.

Making intercession for others is the most powerful and practical way in which we can express our love for them.

JOHN CALVIN

Where there is great love
there are always miracles.
Willa Cather

★

Where there is love and prayer
there is the prower of heaven itself.
Anonymous

Prayers to Pray with Your Children

Pray in the Spirit on all occasions with all kinds of prayers and requests. With this in mind, be alert and always keep on praying for all the saints.

EPHESIANS 6:18

The best way to teach your children to pray is simply to pray with them. This should be a regular, anticipated activity that takes place in your home during good times and bad times and all the in-between times.

If you have been praying for years, it's simply a matter of asking your children to join in with you, remembering that you should keep the activity—holy though it is—consistent with each specific child's age and understanding as demonstrated in the prayers that follow.

If prayer is something new for you, you and your children can learn together, taking turns praying out loud, and discussing the nature of your together prayers.

Resist the excuse that your child is too young or too old to engage in prayer with you. Any age is the right age.

Prayers for the Heart of Your Toddler

A Prayer of Assurance of God's Love and Care

I'm just a child; I have not grown
So very strong or tall
But what I am by you is known
Even though I'm young and small.

You constantly look after me.
Your love is without end.
Never will I doubt or fear
With such a faithful Friend!

A Prayer at Bedtime

Bedtime is the perfect opportunity to pray with your young children. It helps to settle them and prepare them for sleep. It also teaches them to give the last precious moments of their day to God. Memorized prayers are wonderful for toddlers, allowing them to focus on content issues rather than language issues. Long after your children are too old to tuck in, they will remember how good it felt to connect with God at bedtime.

God of Blessing, God of Love,
Watch over us from up above.
God bless Daddy,
God bless Mommy,
God bless . . .
God bless . . .
God bless . . .
And God bless me.
Amen.

Encourage your child to mention everyone in his or her inner circle, including teachers, friends, caregivers, grandparents. It may take a while, but your child is learning to linger in God's presence. Such time is never wasted.

Now I lay me down to sleep,
I pray thee, Lord, my soul to keep;
Thy love be with me through the night
And wake me with the morning light.
Amen.
We thank thee, Lord, for birds and flowers,
For trees and winds and gentle showers.

We thank thee for our clothes and food,
For friends and parents, kind and good.
And, Lord, we thank thee for our play,
And sleep, when tired at close of day.
Amen.

A Prayer at Meals

You will probably be handling the prayers at family meals, but your little ones should be taught to pray even when meals are on the run or away from home.

God is great; God is good.
Let us thank Him for our food.
Amen.

God, bless us with this food you give.
O help each one of us to live
So that Your Blessings and our food
Will do our souls and bodies good.
Amen.

A Morning Prayer of Blessing

Just as important as prayer before going to sleep at night is prayer in the first moments of your child's morning. It puts the day in perspective and establishes the habit of committing the day to God that will follow your children throughout their lives.

Thank you for the sleepy night.
Thank you for the morning light.
Watch over me as I play.
Thank you, Lord, for this fine day.

101

A Prayer of Repentance

Even small children need to confess wrongdoing and receive God's forgiveness. This need not be overly emphasized. Your children may recite the prayer casually or playfully, but over time the message will make its way into their hearts. And you should encourage them with the prayer when they've been disobedient.

There is a sin that leaves a stain
Upon my heart today,
Forgive me, Jesus,
Clean my heart
And take the stain away.
Amen.

A Prayer to Forgive Others

The prayer of forgiveness cannot be learned too soon. Even small children harbor anger and resentment and need to develop the habit of releasing that quickly to God. Insert the name of the offender into the blank.

Dear Jesus:
I have a hurt that's as big as can be.
Touch me, dear Lord, so I can heal.
And help me forgive _____ because
that's your will.
Amen.

A Prayer for Safety

I am God's child,
I'm whole and free;
My God protects and cares for me.
Amen.

God's love fills my mind and heart
And holds me ever near.
I am God's child and have no part
In trouble or in fear.
Amen.

A Prayer for Fear

Dear God,
You are my friend, I know,
And you are always near.
Your love lies in my heart to show
That I can conquer fear.
Amen.

Prayers for Peace

Bless those I love. Bless everyone
With wisdom, peace, and light;
And with tomorrow's rising sun,
God be with us. Good night.
Amen.

My heart is turned all upside down;
I don't know what to do.
Show me how to be at peace
By walking close to you.
Amen.

Prayers When I'm Feeling Sad

Sometimes the clouds fill up the sky
And hide the sun awhile.
But by and by it glows again
With an even bigger smile.
Amen.

Sometimes the clouds fill up my heart
And I feel sad for a while.
But by and by your love for me
Brings back my little smile.
Amen.

Prayers for My Home and Family

Dear Jesus,
Thank you for my home,
Where love and peace are given;
It is the dearest place on earth,
The nearest place to heaven.
Amen.

Thank you for my family,
Bless them, Lord, I pray.
Give them your love and peace
More and more each day.
Amen.

A Prayer for Chores

God, make me happy as I do
The duties that are right.
Teach me to think of others, too,
And make their burdens light.
Then all the many days will come
With goodness that shall bless
Each corner of my heart and home
With love and happiness.
Amen.

105

Prayers for the Heart of Your Elementary-Aged Child

A Prayer at Bedtime

Dear Father,
Thank you for this day and all the ways you have blessed me. I pray for a good night's sleep and peaceful dreams. Watch over my family and send your angels to protect us. Bless all the members of my family and surround us with your presence. I love you, God.
Amen.

A Prayer at Meals

Dear Father,
Thank you for this food I am about to eat. I pray that you would bless it and cause it to nourish and strengthen my body. I pray for hungry people all over the world and ask you to provide for their needs. Bless the hands that have prepared this meal. In Jesus' name.
Amen.

A Prayer Before School

Dear Father,
Before school starts this morning, I pray that you will give the principals and teachers your wisdom, so they can do their jobs well. Help me to learn quickly and do well on my tests. Surround me with your favor, God, and use me to bless others. Fill my school with your love, joy, and peace, and protect every person there. Watch over my family while we are apart.
Amen.

A Prayer for Friendship

Dear God,
I ask you to surround me with godly friends
and protect me from people who would be a
bad influence. I want to be a good friend too.
Help me to be loyal and kind, a person
others can trust. Jesus was a friend to
outcasts, and I ask you to show me the
people who could use a friend like me. Thank
you for being my best friend.
Amen.

107

A Prayer to Receive Christ as Lord and Savior

Dear God,
I want to receive Jesus as my Lord and
Savior. I believe that He was crucified on the
cross and that you raised Him from the
dead. Come into my heart and make me a
new person. Forgive me of my sin, and help
me to please you in what I do and say. Thank
you for making me your child and for loving
me so much. I love you too.
Amen.

A Prayer of Repentance

Dear Father,
I did something I know I shouldn't have
done, and I am sorry. Please forgive me and
wash me clean. If I have hurt others, show
me what to do to make things right. I'm so
thankful that Jesus was punished for my sin
on the cross so that I can be forgiven. Help
me to learn from my mistakes, and help me
not to make them again.
Amen.

108

A Prayer for Protection

Heavenly Father,
The world is such a scary place, and I need
your protection. Only you are big enough to
protect me from all harm. Please give me
your peace and help me not to be afraid. Be
my shield and hide me in your presence.
Assign your angels to watch over me and
keep me safe.
Amen.

A Prayer for Our Nation and Its Leaders

Dear God,
Thank you that my family and I live in a free
country. I pray that you will continue to
bless our nation and cause it to be a godly
influence in the world. I pray for the presi-
dent and all of our national, state, city, and
community leaders. I pray that they would
seek your will and use their positions to
fulfill your plans. Give them wisdom and
protect them from harm.
Amen.

109

A Prayer for Healing

Dear God,
I have come to ask for healing. Your Word
says that Jesus bore our sicknesses and
carried our diseases. It says that by His
wounds we are healed. I receive your
promise by faith, Father, and thank you that
healing is beginning even now. Thank you
for a full recovery. In Jesus' name.
Amen.

A Prayer for Help in School

Dear God,
I'm having a hard time at school right now,
and I need your help. It's scary when I fall
behind, and it embarrasses me in front of
my friends. Help my teacher to explain
things in a way that I can understand. Help
me not to get confused but to think clearly
and catch on quickly. Make me the best
student that I can be.
Amen.

A Prayer to Overcome Rejection

Dear God,
I feel hurt and alone because my friend has
rejected me. When I am not included, it
makes me feel like something is wrong with
me. Thank you for loving me, God. I'm so
glad you will never reject me. Heal my
broken heart and take away the pain. Help
me to forgive those who have hurt me, and
then use me to be a blessing to others who
are hurting.
Amen.

A Prayer to Honor Parents

Dear God,
The Ten Commandments tell me that I am to
honor my parents. I want to do that,
because I know it pleases you and because I
love them. When I am tempted to disobey, to
argue, or to be disrespectful, remind me of
your commandment and give me the
strength to do what is right. Help me to
always be thankful for what they do, and
remind me to tell them.
Amen.

111

A Prayer to Forgive Others

Dear God,
Jesus taught us to love our enemies and
pray for those who hurt us. It is hard, but I
choose to forgive _____ who has
wronged me, just like you forgive me. Help
me to grow in love toward _____,
knowing that your love is big enough for all
of us.
Amen.

A Prayer for Friends and Family

Heavenly Father,
Thank you for my family and friends. I pray
that each person will know Jesus as Lord
and Savior, so someday we can all live
together in heaven. I pray that you will
meet all of their needs. Make their bodies
healthy and strong. When they don't know
what to do, give them wisdom. When they
are sad or lonely, comfort them with your
joy and peace. Watch over them and protect
them, and bless them in every way.
Amen.

112

A Prayer for Guidance

Heavenly Father,
I'm so glad you're such a big God! I ask you
to be my guide. When I don't know what to
do, you always know what is best for me.
Help me make good choices and right deci-
sions. Direct my steps to the people you
want to be in my life. Show me what
hobbies and activities you have planned for
me. Help me develop my talents for your
glory. Guide everything I do.
Amen.

A Prayer for Peace

Dear God,
I need your peace. I feel all upset inside, and
I know that isn't the way you want me to
feel. Show me if I've done something wrong
so that I can do something about it and I can
have your peace again. Show me if my heart
is full of fear so that I can put my trust in
you again. I know that's how to have peace.
Amen.

113

A Prayer When Your Child Is Feeling Sad

Dear Father,
I'm really sad about something. I know that
you know all about it, and that makes me
feel better. You sent the Holy Spirit to be our
comforter, and that is what I need. Help me
to sense your presence and to feel your love.
Take my sadness away and fill me with your
joy. Then lead me to others who are sad, so I
can point them to you.
Amen.

Prayers for the Heart of Your Teen

A Prayer at Bedtime

Dear Father,
I thank you for every good thing that happened today, because I know that you are the source of it all. Give me a good night's sleep with pleasant dreams, so I'll be ready to tackle tomorrow rested and ready to serve you. I pray for your blessing upon every family member and thank you for watching over us all—for guiding and protecting us and for leading us in your will.
Amen.

A Prayer at Meals

Heavenly Father,
Thank you for this meal I am about to eat. I don't take it for granted, but recognize it as part of your generous provision. I realize that there are hungry people all over the world, and I ask you to supply their needs for nutritious meals as well. Bless this food to the nourishment and strength of my body, and bless the hands that prepared it.
Amen.

A Prayer Before School

Good morning, God!
I pray for my teachers, principals, and
bosses—that you would give them wisdom
today to do their jobs well. I pray that my
mind will be alert and that you will enable
me to do my very best. Grant me favor with
the many people who cross my path today,
and use me to bless them. Order my steps
and cause everything to work together for
my good and your glory.
Amen.

A Prayer of Repentance

Dear God,
I really blew it—again. I'm truly sorry, and I
ask you to forgive me. Thank you for your
promise to cleanse me of all sin and to give
me a fresh start. I'm so grateful that you
don't condemn me but always believe the
best. Thank you for second chances and for
giving me the grace to walk free from sin.
I'm thankful that nothing can separate me
from your love.
Amen.

A Prayer to Forgive Others

Heavenly Father,
I know you want me to forgive, but it's so
hard! I need your help to "turn the other
cheek." Thank you for filling my heart with
your love. I choose to extend that love to
the one who has wronged me. I do forgive,
just as you have forgiven me. By your grace,
cause my feelings to catch up to my deci-
sion so that my heart will be truly free.
Amen.

A Prayer for Friends and Family

Heavenly Father,
Thank you for the awesome family and
friends you've given me. For those who
haven't received Jesus as their Lord and
Savior, I pray that you will open their eyes to
see the truth. Protect each of these people
who mean so much to me. Meet all of their
needs—spirit, soul, and body—and grant
them your peace. May they all be filled with
your amazing love.
Amen.

A Prayer to Receive Christ as Lord and Savior

Dear God,
I realize that this is the biggest decision I will ever make, and I am ready to make it. I acknowledge that Jesus is your Son, born of the virgin Mary. I believe that He hung on the cross to pay for my sin and that you raised Him from the dead. I make Jesus my Lord and Savior. Take my life and do something with it. I love you, Father.
Amen.

117

A Prayer for the Nation

Heavenly Father,
Thank you for allowing my family and me to live in a free country. I pray for our president and all of the leaders at every level of government. Give them wisdom to do their jobs well and fill their hearts with a desire to do your will. You said that if we would humble ourselves and pray that you would heal our land. I ask you to do that, Father, that our country may glorify you.
Amen.

A Prayer for Guidance

Heavenly Father,
I ask you to be my Guide, to order my steps,
to lead me in your ways so that I can experi-
ence your full blessing. As I read your Word, I
ask the Holy Spirit to enlighten my eyes so
that I can see what you want me to see.
Cause my paths to grow brighter and
brighter, and alert me if I ever begin to
stray. Keep me on track for your glory.
Amen.

A Prayer for Safety

Father,
If I let myself, I could become a very fearful
person, but instead I turn to you. Only you
can truly keep me safe, and I choose to dwell
in you and walk in your ways. Thank you for
assigning angels to watch over me. Protect
me from deadly sickness, thieves, and
violence. Shelter me when threatening
weather strikes. Keep me safe in the palm of
your hand as I rest secure in you.
Amen.

A Prayer for Peace

Heavenly Father,
I need the "peace that passes understand-
ing" that your Word talks about. I thank you
that Jesus is my Prince of Peace; and as I
focus my attention on you, my heart and
mind become still. To obey your Word, I dwell
on things that are good, true, and positive,
knowing that you are working everything
out for the best. Thank you for your peace,
regardless of what is going on around me.
Amen.

119

A Prayer for Healing

Dear God,
You are so awesome! To think that Jesus bore
my sickness on the cross along with my sin!
It's amazing. By Jesus' stripes, I am healed
and made whole. The same Spirit that raised
Christ from the dead now lives in me, and it
drives out sickness and fills my body with
life.
Amen.

A Prayer for Help at School

Heavenly Father,
I'm really struggling at school right now,
and I need your help. Give me favor with my
teachers and help them to explain things in
a way that I can understand. Cause my mind
to be sharp, and help me retain what I learn.
Give me favor with my friends and other
students. Show me what I can do to make
my school experience more positive. Thank
you for turning this situation around.
Amen.

120

A Prayer When Your Teen Is Depressed

God,
I am really down. Nothing is going right, and
it's like I'm walking through quicksand and
have no energy. There's a gray cloud hanging
over me and I'm not sure I'll ever see the sun
again. Actually, I'm afraid I won't. You are
my only hope, God. Be the miracle worker
that you are, and turn things around for me.
Open my eyes to see what you see so that I
can smile again.
Amen.

A Prayer When Your Teen Is Lonely

God,
I'm so lonely. Even in the midst of a crowd, I
feel like I don't fit in. Comfort my heart,
Father, and help me to recognize your pres-
ence. I know you want me to have friends
who love you like I do. Lead me to them, and
give me a place to belong. Then show me
others who are lonely and give me the
courage to reach out.
Amen.

121

Pray daily for your children and
don't be afraid to let them
see you on your knees.

Anonymous

Prayers for Your Child's Specific Needs

Every time you cross my mind,
I break out in exclamations of thanks to God.
Each exclamation is a trigger to prayer. I find myself
praying for you with a glad heart.

PHILIPPIANS 1:3-4

Prayers for the Needs of Your Toddler

A Prayer When Dealing With Sickness

Dear Lord,
My little one is hurting. I've done everything
I can do, but only you can make my child
completely well and whole. Touch the
precious little body before me. Make it
whole and healthy. Thank you for your faith-
ful and watchful care over my child.
Amen.

A Prayer When Dealing With Anger

Dear Father,
My precious little one has quite a temper. I
can see the human nature rising up. Give me
the wisdom to deal with this tendency in a
way that will serve my child well in life and
in relationship with you. Give me the
patience to respond calmly when provoked
by disobedience and tantrums. And show me
how to discipline in a way that is pleasing
to you.
Amen.

A Prayer When Dealing With Danger

Dear Lord,
Keep my eyes and ears open and my mind
focused on the job you have given me—the
physical care of my child. Warn me when
danger is near and help me to know how to
keep my little one out of harm's way. And
when I've done all I can, help me to leave the
rest to you—the one who sees all and knows
all.
Amen.

A Prayer for Your Toddler's Healthy Self-Image

Dear Lord,
I spend all my time with this sweet, little
one. Help me to always be encouraging, even
when that includes discipline. Show me how
to draw out my child's gifts and talents and
not focus on weaknesses and flaws. Most of
all, help me to constantly be reminding my
child that you are the great Creator—and
all you create is good.
Amen.

A Prayer When Dealing With Separation

Dear Father,
My little one is so attached to me that when I have to be away—even for a few minutes—panic takes over. Show me how to comfort and assure my child that you are always there even when I'm not. You are always watching until I quickly come back again.
Amen.

126

A Prayer When There Is Fear and Anxiety

Dear Father,
We live in a frightening world, full of unknown evil. Show me how to instill a sense of security in my child despite this truth. Give me the right balance as I strive to keep my child safe in a way that will discourage fear and anxiety and instill confidence and trust.
Amen.

Prayers for the Needs of Your Elementary-Aged Child

A Prayer When Dealing With Sickness

Heavenly Father,
Few things hurt my heart more than when
my children are sick or in pain. It must hurt
your heart too, since you laid our infirmities
on Jesus along with our sin. I am so thankful
that Jesus is the Great Physician. I'm asking
Him to make a house call today! May
healing flow to my children and drive out
every trace of sickness, weakness, or pain, in
Jesus' name.
Amen.

127

A Prayer When Dealing With Anger

Heavenly Father,
Anger is such a difficult emotion to deal
with. Show me healthy ways to deal with it
myself so that I can be an example for my
children. Help my children not to hurt others
with their anger, but also help them not to
hold anger inside, which will only hurt them.
Encourage my children to turn to you and
exchange their anger for your love, forgive-
ness, and peace. Help them—and me—to
love and forgive like you do.
Amen.

A Prayer When Dealing With Depression

Heavenly Father,
I'm really concerned about depression in my
children. Expose the root of the problem, so
we can deal with it. Grant me wisdom and
insight into what I can do to help, and give
me words that will encourage and inspire
hope. Fill my children with your joy, Father,
and give them a glimpse into the wonderful
future you have for them. Let them know
how very special they are to you.
Amen.

A Prayer When Dealing With Loneliness

Heavenly Father,
We all feel lonely at times, but I hate to see
it in my children. Show us things that we
can do as a family, so that each child feels
significant. Bring godly friends into their
lives, and give them the courage to reach
out to others. Most of all, comfort their
hearts with the fact that you will never
leave them nor forsake them. Because of
you, they are never alone.
Amen.

A Prayer When Dealing With Discouragement

Heavenly Father,
When I see my children discouraged, it
breaks my heart. I want to rush in and make
everything okay, but I can't always do that.
Whether it is through my words, the words
of others, or directly from you, encourage
the hearts of my children. Help them to see
the positive, and fill them with a confident
expectation for the good things you have in
store for them. Thank you, Father.
Amen.

129

A Prayer When Dealing With Rebellion

Heavenly Father,
Rebellion in my children makes me angry
and afraid. I need your help! Only you can
touch their hearts in a way that can
produce lasting change. Draw them by your
love to all that is good and right. Give them
a hunger for your Word. Bring godly friends
into their lives, and orchestrate circum-
stances to bring about your purposes. Let
them know that they are loved—by you and
by me—and that nothing can ever change
that.
Amen.

A Prayer When Dealing With Guidance

Heavenly Father,
To be a good parent, I am utterly dependent
upon your guidance. My vision is so limited,
but you see the big picture. I'm confident
that you have a wonderful plan established
for my children. Be their Guide, Father, so
they can walk in your ways. Cause your
Word to light their path, and give me the
wisdom I need to help them on their way.
Amen.

130

A Prayer When Dealing With Danger

Heavenly Father,
Being a parent today can be so scary!
Whether it is crime, disease, terrorism, or
even the weather, it seems that danger is
lurking around every corner. But you said
not to be afraid. The only way I can do that
is to totally rely on you for the safety of my
children. Give your angels charge over them,
Father. Deliver them from evil. Guide their
steps, and be their shield.
Amen.

A Prayer When There Is Trouble at School

Heavenly Father,
Sometimes I feel utterly helpless when it
comes to my children having trouble at
school, mainly because I can't always be
with them. I'm so thankful that you are!
Give them favor with their teachers and
peers. Help them to resolve conflicts. Cause
their minds to be sharp and alert, quick to
grasp new concepts and able to retain them.
Keep my children safe, and cause everything
to work for their good.
Amen.

A Prayer When There Are Problem Relationships

Heavenly Father,
I'm very concerned about some of my chil-
dren's relationships. First, I pray that you
will work in the lives of the people who are
having a negative influence so that they
will walk in your ways. But if they resist, I
pray that you will remove them from my
children's lives. Surround my children with
godly friends who will influence them posi-
tively. Give my children the strength to
serve you wholeheartedly.
Amen.

A Prayer When Dealing With Separation

Heavenly Father,
Separation anxiety is heartrending. To feel
my children holding on to me for dear life, to
hear them crying, to see their arms reaching
out as I have to break away is almost more
than I can stand. Comfort my children,
Father. Fill them with your peace so that
fear won't take hold of their hearts. Give
them the assurance that we will be together
again soon. Give them courage and strength.
Amen.

132

A Prayer When It's Time to Leave Home

Heavenly Father,
I don't know who takes it harder, my chil-
dren or me, when it's time for them to leave
home. To be such a healthy part of life, it
sure can be painful. Help us all to trust you
during these times of transition. Multiply
your grace and peace in our hearts so that
we don't get entangled in anxiety or sorrow.
Remind us that we will always be in one
another's hearts.
Amen.

A Prayer When There Is Fear and Anxiety

Heavenly Father,
"Fear not." You said that so many times in
your Word. You knew how much we would
need to hear it. When my children are
anxious, help me to point them to you. Lead
us to scriptures that will dispel fear and fill
my children with courage and peace. There
is nothing they cannot face with you at
their side. Cause them to see themselves as
more than conquerors through Christ.
Amen.

133

A Prayer to Hunger for God and Grow Spiritually

Heavenly Father,
There are many things that I want for my
children, but the most important is that
they hunger for you and grow spiritually. I
want them to experience to the full the
abundant life you've planned for them. Help
me to set a good example by having an
exciting and fulfilling walk with you myself,
and whet their appetites for the things of
heaven so that they will never settle for
less.
Amen.

A Prayer to Become More Responsible

Heavenly Father,
Becoming a responsible adult doesn't come
automatically, and the road to get there is
often difficult. No one knows my children
like you do, Father, and I covet your wisdom
as I train them to accept more and more
responsibility. Give them a desire to grow,
and give me the insight I need for their indi-
vidual personalities. I want to help them
reach their full potential so their lives will
glorify you.
Amen.

134

A Prayer for Godly Friends

Heavenly Father,
I believe I am having an eternal impact on
my children, but the older they become, the
more their friends can influence them.
Surround each of my children with godly
friends whose parents have similar values
to ours. I pray that these children will
encourage one another in their walk with
you and support one another in taking a
stand for godliness. Finally, use them to
bring revival to their peer group.
Amen.

A Prayer for a Blessed Future

Heavenly Father,
I am encouraged by your promise that you
have good plans for each of my children, an
abundant life that is more fulfilling than
anything they can ask, think, or imagine.
Instead of allowing anything from the past
to discourage them about the future, may
they hold fast to your promises. Open their
eyes to the exciting things you have
planned, and give them the courage never to
settle for less than your will.
Amen.

135

A Prayer for Your Child's Future Mate

Heavenly Father,
I pray for the young people whom you have
chosen to marry my children. May they be
raised in godly homes and become believers
at an early age. Steer them toward godly
influences and deliver them from evil. Help
them to resist sexual sin and to keep them-
selves pure till marriage. Keep them healthy
and whole, and when the time is right, bless
them with marriages that will always honor
you.
Amen.

A Prayer for Your Child's Healthy Self-Image

Heavenly Father,
Having a healthy self-image is so important to success in life, and I pray that you will help my children grow to become secure adults. Give me wisdom so that I can parent them in a way that always builds up and never tears down. Help me to love them unconditionally so that they always feel valued. Most of all, Father, help them to see themselves as you see them, priceless with unlimited potential.
Amen.

Prayers for the Needs of Your Teen

A Prayer When Dealing With Sickness

Heavenly Father,
I hate it when my children are sick. There is only so much I can do to help them get better, but I can—and do—look to you, the Source of healing. Give me wisdom about medications that can help and to know whether or not we should go to the doctor. Quicken my child's body as you fill it with your healing virtue. Restore vitality and strength. Thank you for your healing promises.
Amen.

137

A Prayer When Dealing With Anger

Dear God,
Anger is such an unpleasant emotion. When my children get angry, I just want to shut them down, but that isn't always healthy. Give me wisdom so that I can teach my children how to deal with anger in a godly way. Help me equip them with positive communication skills so that they can resolve conflict. Help them learn to exercise self-control and look to you to settle their emotions.
Amen.

A Prayer When Dealing With Depression

Heavenly Father,
I am really concerned about depression in
my children. I've tried to help them snap out
of it, but that doesn't always work. Surround
my children with your presence, and heal
their broken hearts. Comfort them and fill
them with your joy. Give them a song in
their hearts and a bounce in their steps.
Help them to see things from your perspec-
tive, and assure them that good things are
on the horizon.
Amen.

A Prayer When Dealing With Loneliness

Heavenly Father,
The teenage years are so hard. I remember
what it was like to feel lonely, like I didn't
fit in. Give my children good Christian
friends with whom they can share matters
of the heart. Lead them to activities that
will fill them with purpose and satisfy their
need to belong. But most of all, help them to
sense your presence, because you are the
Friend who sticks closer than a brother.
Amen.

A Prayer When Dealing With Discouragement

Heavenly Father,
*Oh, how I wish I had a magic wand that could make everything okay. But I have something—someone—even better: **You.** You truly are a miracle worker, and your Word brings hope to even the most hopeless situation. Give me words of encouragement that will jump-start my children's spirits. Reveal your faithfulness to them, and give them confidence that you are at work in their situation, turning it around for good.*
Amen.

A Prayer When Dealing With Rebellion

Heavenly Father,
When I see rebellion in my children, it scares me. Where will it end? Since you made my children, I look to you to show me how to most effectively handle this destructive attitude. Soften hard hearts and give my children a desire to please you and walk in your ways. Replace unhealthy relationships with godly ones, and rearrange circum-stances to lead my children to your path for their lives.
Amen.

A Prayer When Dealing With Guidance

Heavenly Father,
I used to make all of the decisions for my
children when they were small, but now
they are making decisions for themselves,
some that could alter their lives perma-
nently. I trust you to be their guide, to direct
them into your perfect will for their lives. I
pray that they will know your voice, and if
they ever begin to choose a wrong path,
alert them by your Spirit.
Amen.

A Prayer When Dealing With Danger

Heavenly Father,
Your Word tells me not to be afraid, but
that's hard right now because danger is
afoot. You love my children even more than I
do, so I trust you to protect them. If neces-
sary, miraculously deliver them. Thank you
for surrounding them with angels and
hiding them under the shadow of your
wings. Send my children exactly what they
need, when they need it, and bring them to a
place of safety.
Amen.

A Prayer When Dealing With Addiction

Heavenly Father,
My children thought they could control it,
but now they've been ensnared by addiction
and it is threatening to destroy them. I pray
that the same Spirit that raised Christ from
the dead would quicken their bodies and
drive out addiction and its cravings. Give my
children the strength to overcome, and give
them wisdom on how not to fall prey to
addiction again. Help them develop healthy
desires, behaviors, habits, and friendships.
Amen.

141

A Prayer When There Is Trouble at School

Heavenly Father,
My children are having trouble at school
and need your help. I can't be there all the
time, but you are. When they need help
from the faculty, I pray you will give them
the courage to ask. Cause their minds to be
sharp and catch on quickly in their
academics. Be at the center of all their
relationships with peers and give them
favor. Guide them to whatever help they
need.
Amen.

A Prayer When There Are Problem Relationships

Heavenly Father,
I am concerned about some of my children's
relationships and the negative influences I
see. Work in the hearts of these people and
my children so they can develop healthy
attitudes and behaviors. If necessary,
remove ungodly friends and send new
Christian ones in their place. Give my chil-
dren wisdom to make good choices that are
in keeping with your will for their lives. May
all their relationships be holy and pleasing
to you.
Amen.

A Prayer When It's Time to Leave Home

Heavenly Father,
I knew this day would come, but so quickly?
I pray that I've invested enough into my
children. I trust you to make up the differ-
ence. Help us to get through this transition
time smoothly, to cut each other slack, to be
supportive and kind. Help us to treasure the
past but embrace this new chapter. We may
be apart physically, but help us to always
stay close in our hearts.
Amen.

A Prayer When There Is Fear and Anxiety

Heavenly Father,
I am concerned about my children. Fear and
anxiety are threatening their well-being, so
I intercede for them. Cause your perfect love
to drive out these crippling emotions, and
replace them with your gentle peace. Fill
them with the assurance that you are with
them, to calm the storm in their hearts. May
their trust in you grow to a new and deeper
level.
Amen.

143

A Prayer to Hunger for God and Grow Spiritually

Heavenly Father,
The thing I want most for my children is for
them to know you personally and walk in
your ways. Give them a hunger for your
Word and your presence. Show them how to
put you first and to keep worldly things in
perspective. Help them to recognize your
voice. Keep them on their appointed path.
Empower them to faithfully serve you all of
their days and to bear fruit to further your
kingdom.
Amen.

A Prayer to Become More Responsible

Heavenly Father,
It's ironic that my children want the free-
doms of adulthood but not the responsibili-
ties. I suppose it's human nature, but it's
time to grow up. Cause what they've been
taught to take root and produce fruit. Give
them a desire to do what is right and to
leave childish ways behind. Provide oppor-
tunities for them to embrace their responsi-
bilities and then bless them for their efforts.
Help them to become everything you've
designed.
Amen.

A Prayer for Godly Friends

Heavenly Father,
There is a battle going on for the souls of my
children, and they could easily be influenced
by the wrong crowd. Give them an arsenal of
good, godly friends with whom they can
walk in your ways. Light a fire in their
hearts and help them to become totally sold
out to you. Make them a force for positive
change in their school and use them to bring
revival.
Amen.

144

A Prayer for a Blessed Future

Heavenly Father,
As a parent, I could easily worry about my
children's future, but I look to you to be Lord
of their lives. By your Spirit, guide them in
your ways. Lead them to the good life you've
planned for them, that place of greatest
blessing that is exceedingly abundantly
above all we can think or imagine. I trust
you to bring about your perfect will for their
lives. Thank you, Father.
Amen.

A Prayer for Your Teen's Future Mate

Heavenly Father,
You already know who you have planned for
my children to marry, and I pray they will
never settle for less. Work in both my chil-
dren and their future mates so they will be
compatible and bring out the best in one
another. Protect them from counterfeits, and
give them the strength to stay pure till they
wed. In your timing, orchestrate a holy
courtship, and give them a marriage made
in heaven.
Amen.

Prayer is not the fruit of natural talents;
it is the product of faith, of holiness,
of deeply spiritual character.
Men learn to pray as they learn to love.
Perfection in simplicity, in humility, in faith—
these form its chief ingredients.

EDWARD MCKENDREE BOUNDS

Scripture Prayers

All Scripture is God-breathed and is useful for teaching, rebuking, correcting and training in righteousness, so that the man of God may be thoroughly equipped for every good work.

2 Timothy 3:16–17

There is a wonderful advantage to praying the words of God as recorded in the Bible over your children—no matter what age they might be. Even when the words were spoken by Solomon or Paul or any of the other individuals who penned the sacred Scriptures, they are God-inspired and as such you can be certain that they fall within the will of God. What a beautiful and pure way to pray for your children. Just insert your child's name in the blank.

A Prayer for Salvation

Dear Lord,
I know that it is your desire for all, including
_____, to be saved and come to a knowl-
edge of the truth (1 Timothy 2:3–4).
I pray that _____ would come to believe
in Jesus Christ, and will therefore receive
forgiveness of sins through His name (Acts
10:43). I thank you for becoming the Source
of eternal salvation for _____ as
(he/she) obeys you (Hebrews 5:9).
Amen.

A Prayer for Success

Dear Lord,
I pray that you would give _____
the desire of (his/her) heart and make all
(his/her) plans succeed (Psalm 20:4). Show
_____ that success comes by being
careful to observe your laws. Impress upon
_____ that there is no reason to be
afraid or discouraged, but rather strong and
courageous (1 Chronicles 22:13).
Amen.

A Prayer for God's Will

Dear Father,
I ask you to transform _____ by the
renewing of (his/her) mind that (he/she)
might be able to test and approve what your
will is—your good, pleasing, and perfect
will (Romans 12:2). Help _____ to rightly
understand that the world and its desires
will pass away, but the person who does
your will surely will live forever
(1 John 2:17).
Amen.

A Prayer for Wisdom and Discernment

Dear Father,
When _____ lacks wisdom, I pray that
(he/she) will ask you for it, because I know
that you will give it generously and without
finding fault (James 1:5). My own wisdom is
nothing compared to yours. Because it
comes down from heaven, it is first of all
pure; then peace-loving, considerate,
submissive, full of mercy and good fruit,
impartial, and sincere (James 3:17).
Amen.

A Prayer for Self-Control

Dear Lord,
Teach _____ self-control, because Satan,
our enemy, is always prowling around
looking for someone to devour
(1 Peter 5:8). Thank you that no temptation
will seize _____ that is not common to all
human beings. And thank you that you are
faithful, unwilling to let _____ be
tempted beyond what (he/she) is able to
bear. And most of all, Lord, thank you for
always providing a way out so that
_____ can stand up against it (1
Corinthians 10:13).
Amen.

A Prayer for Character

Dear Lord,
I ask that you endow _____ with a
strong conscience that motivates (him/her)
to behave in a godly manner in this world,
especially in relation to others. Help
(him/her) to grow in the holiness and sincer-
ity that are from you. And thank you for
giving (him/her) the grace needed to do so (2
Corinthians 1:12).
Amen.

151

A Prayer for Protection

Dear Lord,
Be a hiding place for _____. Protect
(him/her) in trouble and surround (him/her)
with songs of deliverance (Psalm 32:7).
Thank you, Lord, for you are faithful. You will
strengthen and protect _____ from the
evil one (2 Thessalonians 3:3).
Amen.

A Prayer for Purpose in Life

Dear Lord,
I know that you have a plan for _____, a
plan that will cause (him/her) to prosper, a
plan that will keep (him/her) from harm,
and a plan that will give (him/her) hope and
a future (Jeremiah 29:11). Remind me to
encourage _____ and build (him/her) up
in this truth (1 Thessalonians 5:11).
Amen.

152

A Prayer for Integrity

Dear Lord,
Help me in everything to set an example for
_____ by doing what is good. Guide me as
I teach with integrity, seriousness, and
soundness of speech so that (he/she) will not
be ashamed because no one will have
anything bad to say about (him/her) (Titus
2:7–8). Thank you, Lord, that when I teach
_____ to walk in integrity, I am giving
(him/her) the opportunity to walk securely,
even in this dangerous world (Proverbs
10:9).
Amen.

Arrow Prayers

Have some arrow prayers to pray during the day, or a psalm. A good watchmaker is one who makes watches and prays; a good housemaid is one who sweeps and prays.

E. B. Pusey

Arrow Prayers

→ *Remember your mercies, Lord.*

→ *Be gracious to me, O God.*

→ *In you I hope all day long.*

→ *In your love remember me.*

→ *In you I place all my trust.*

→ *Awake, O my soul, awake!*

→ *Create a clean heart in me.*

→ *Have mercy on me, O God.*

→ *Glory to the Lamb of God.*

→ *Holy, holy, holy Lord.*

→ *You are my strength and my song.*

→ *The Lord keeps the little ones.*

→ *How good is the Lord of all.*

→ *Fill me with joy and gladness.*

→ *Let the healing waters flow.*

→ *Oh, that we might know the Lord!*

→ *Let go and let God.*

Five Grand Conditions of Prevailing Prayer:

★ Complete dependence upon the merits and mediation of the Lord Jesus Christ, as the only grounds of any claim for blessing.

★ Separation from all known sin.

★ Faith in God's Word of promise.

★ Asking in accordance with God's will.

★ There must be waiting *on* God and waiting *for* God.

The Lord's Prayer

Our Father, who art in heaven,
Hallowed be thy name.

Thy kingdom come, thy will be done
On earth as it is in heaven.

Give us this day our daily bread
And forgive us our trespasses
As we forgive those who trespass against us.

Lead us not into temptation,
But deliver us from evil.

For thine is the kingdom
And the power
And the glory
Forever.

Amen.

The Parent's Response to the Lord's Prayer

Dear Lord:

*I cannot say **our***
If I make no room for my children and their needs.

*I cannot say **Father***
If I do not demonstrate this relationship before my children in my daily living.

*I cannot say **who art in heaven***
If all my interests and pursuits are on earthly things rather than my children's eternal good.

*I cannot say **hallowed be thy name***
If I, who am called by His name, am not holy before my children.

*I cannot say **thy kingdom come***
If I am unwilling to give up my own sovereignty and accept the righteous reign of God in my children's lives.

*I cannot say **thy will be done***
If I am unwilling or resentful of those things God has called me to do on behalf of my children.

*I cannot say **in earth as it is in heaven***
Unless I am truly ready to give myself in His service to my children.

*I cannot say **give us this day our daily bread***

Without committing myself to prayer on behalf of my children's needs.

*I cannot say **forgive us our trespasses as we forgive those who trespass against us** If I continue to harbor a grudge against one of my children.*

*I cannot say **lead us not into temptation** If I carelessly allow them to be placed in situations where they will face temptation before they are strong enough to handle it.*

*I cannot say **deliver us from evil** If I am not prepared to fight in the spiritual realm with the weapon of prayer on behalf of my children.*

*I cannot say **thine is the kingdom** If I do not give the King the respect He deserves in our home.*

*I cannot say **thine is the power** If I fear being persecuted because I am raising my children in God's ways.*

*I cannot say **thine is the glory** If I am seeking my own glory through the lives of my children.*

*I cannot say **forever** If I am too anxious about each day's affairs to trust God to care for my children.*

*I cannot say **amen** Unless I can honestly say, "Cost what it may, this is my prayer."*

Resources

Books

Prayer Starters for Busy Moms: How to Pray All Day and Still Put the Laundry Away by Tracy Klehn

Listening Prayer: Learning to Hear God's Voice and Keep a Prayer Journal by Leanne Payne

Teach Me to Pray by Andrew Murray

31 Days of Prayer for My Teen: A Parent's Guide by Susan Alexander Yates

A Mother's Prayers for Her Children by Nancy Ann Yaeger

Little Girls' Book of Prayers for Mothers and Daughters by Carolyn Larsen

The Pocket Guide for Parents: Raising Godly Kids

Web sites

★ *When We Pray* Web site: *www.whenwepray.com/index.html*. Includes free *When Mothers Pray* Bible study download, articles on praying with your children, and examples of answered prayer. Also lists books by Cheri Fuller on praying with your children and teens.

★ *PrayKids!* magazine. Information about and sample issue at *www.navpress.com/Magazines/PrayKids/*

★ Article titled "Praying With Children: Parents can guide youngsters in expressing their natural spirituality" by Sharon Sheridan at *www.episcopalchurch.org/26769_53350_ENG_HTM.htm*

★ Article titled "Way to Pray! How to make the ACTS prayer method accessible to your child" by Greg Asimakoupoulos at *www.christianitytoday.com/cpt/2005/001/9.38.html*

★ Article titled "31 Biblical Virtues to Pray for Your Kids" by Bob Hostetler at *www.labc.com/children/page.php?id=159*

★ Web site dedicated to kids' prayer: *www.kidsprayer.com/*

★ *Kids Praying for Kids,* free twelve-month prayer journal for children ages 6–10, which tells about kids in desperate situations around the world. Available through Samaritan's Purse Canada at *www.samaritanspurse.ca/occ/prayer_network/kids_praying_for_kids.aspx*

★ Web site for The Presidential Prayer Team for Kids: *www.pptkids.org/index.php*. This is a nonprofit organization devoted to teaching children to pray for the president and other leaders. Weekly issues include interesting articles for kids about leaders in the news, the spiritual roots of our founding fathers, and Bible verses pertaining to prayer.

★ Web site *www.kidsinneedofprayer.com/* dedicated to children praying for one another. Author of site is an eleven-year-old child who was born with a cocaine addiction but was miraculously delivered as a result of prayer. Includes the child's testimony. Children can communicate prayer requests and post answers to prayer, as well as learn of other children in need of prayer.

★ Lengthy article titled "Teaching Children to Pray" at *www.nethomeschool.com/teachingchildrentopray.htm*. Includes basic principles to teach children how to pray plus suggestions of practical things children can do to develop their prayer life. Article also includes extensive list of books, organizations, videos, and other resource materials devoted to prayer.

★ Article titled "10 Things Children Should Know About Prayer" by Susan Taylor Brown at *www.susan taylorbrown.com/prayer.html*. Brief description of ten important prayer points that are easy for children to grasp. May dispel misconceptions children have about prayer.

★ Learn about See You at the Pole, a student-initiated, student-organized, and student-led gathering of students meeting at their school flagpole to pray for their school, teachers, friends, government, and nation. It is not a demonstration or political rally, but simply a prayer gathering. For more information, go to *www.syatp.com/info/basics.html*

★ Article titled "Let the Children Pray" by Eric Reed about Brooklyn Tabernacle's powerful children's prayer meetings. Go to *www.christianitytoday.com/tc/2002/002/4.14.html*